CAMBRIDGE SERMONS

BY

EDWYN CLEMENT HOSKYNS, *Bart.*, M.C.

Fellow, Dean of Chapel, and Librarian of Corpus Christi College,
Cambridge: Hon. D.D. (St Andrews) : Honorary Canon of Derby

with an appreciation by
CHARLES SMYTH

S·P·C·K

LONDON

First published in 1938
Large Paperback edition 1970
S.P.C.K.
Holy Trinity Church
Marylebone Road
London N.W.1

Made and printed offset in Great Britain by
The Camelot Press Ltd, London and Southampton

SBN 281 02494 4

PUBLISHER'S NOTE

Sir Edwyn Hoskyns died in 1937, yet the three chief books with which his name is connected are still in print—*The Riddle of the New Testament* (with F. N. Davey) 1931; his translation of Karl Barth's *Epistle to the Romans* (1933); and his *Fourth Gospel*, edited by F. N. Davey, 1940. This is more than many theologians have left to keep their memories green thirty-three years after their deaths. But, by themselves, these three books do not give a complete impression of Hoskyns's interests and intellectual output. It was said of him, in Cambridge, that his lectures were sermons, and his sermons lectures. That did not mean that they were similar in texture or technique—far from it. But few left his lectures without feeling stimulated to fresh study of the New Testament as an urgent spiritual duty; and few listened to his sermons without feeling they were being admitted to an essentially scholarly discussion and argument—a discussion and argument which involved the layman as well as the priest. There is still in print a small volume of other sermons by Hoskyns—*We are the Pharisees*—but it is this first collection of *Cambridge Sermons*, admirably chosen and introduced by Canon Charles Smyth, which most successfully supplies the complement to his major works of scholarship; and still helps to give a more complete impression of the scope and method which made him remarkable both for the diversity of his interests and for the originality of his insights.

July 1970

CONTENTS

EDWYN CLEMENT HOSKYNS

1884–1937

For many of my generation—that is, the generation that
began to take an interest in public affairs about 1911, or
later (and therefore just missed the impact of Tyrrell,
Von Hügel, Schweitzer, or Scott Holland, to mention
no others), the two outstanding names in the history of
Christian thought in England in the present century are
those of G. K. Chesterton and Sir Edwyn Hoskyns.

Their respective tasks differed as widely as their
methods. Of all that was romantic and superficial in
Chesterton, Hoskyns was, in point of fact, instinctively
distrustful; while Chesterton would probably have been
no less suspicious of the pure scholarship of Hoskyns.
Yet both alike were men by whom God wrought great
deliverance from the tyranny of superstition: and it is
for that deliverance that we, who have entered into their
labours, owe to their memories an incalculable debt.

It was given to Chesterton, more than to any other
single individual, to change the intellectual climate of
his age. He belonged, as he himself remarks in his
Autobiography, to the generation that was educated by
agnostics: and he became the ringleader in what was in
truth something between a mutiny and a war of libera-
tion, and yet which never seemed quite to lose the spirit
of an undergraduate rag. That was indeed the secret both
of its strength and of its weakness. The one limitation of
Chesterton's apologetic was that, despite its brilliant
fencing and its intellectual exuberance, it lacked the

foundation of a solid and well-knit theology. Yet he was able to demonstrate with a wealth of paradox and with an enormous sense of fun that if anything was stuffy and pedantic and intellectually obsolete and obscurantist and dreary and second-rate, it was not the Christian Religion, but the procession of religions and philosophies that claimed to be intellectually and morally superior to Christianity. His bowling was so unconventional, according to the decorous standards of the devout agnostic, that conventional agnosticism, the ethical rationalism of that age of refined but muddled thinking, was quite unable to stand up to it. The result is that at the present time the Christian side is in, and has in fact been batting for a considerable period. For it is partly thanks to the lobs and yorkers and full-pitchers of Chestertonian apologetic that to-day it is generally admitted to be intellectually respectable to call yourself a Christian: which was perhaps a more disputable proposition thirty years ago.

The particular tyranny of superstition from which it was given to Hoskyns to deliver us was not the tyranny of ethical rationalism, but rather the tyranny of that Liberal Humanitarianism in which old-fashioned agnosticism had naturally tended to take refuge. His essay on *The Christ of the Synoptic Gospels* in *Essays Catholic and Critical* (ed. E. G. Selwyn, 1926), which carried his reputation far beyond the limits of the Cambridge Divinity School, may be said to have marked, chronologically, the turning of the tide in the study of New Testament theology in England. In that epoch-making essay, Hoskyns demonstrated overwhelmingly that 'the Jesus of History' was not the Jesus of history at all. Let it be said at once that no estimate of its significance would be fair or just that omitted to mention the influence of Schweitzer's *Von Reimarus zu Wrede* (English tr. 1910, *The Quest of the Historical Jesus*) which lay behind it. Yet Hoskyns' essay, if it did not initiate, undoubtedly contributed to ensure the victory of a constructive Liberal Catholicism that was Evangelical in its very essence, over the popularised Liberal Protestant interpretation of the Gospels. It is easy now to forget the importance of that essay at the moment of its publication: but if its value after the passage of a decade is no longer so conspicuous as it was in 1926, that is in itself a silent tribute to its effectiveness.

Hoskyns had studied under Harnack at Berlin before the War: he was a friend of Schweitzer: at a later period he had the honour of lecturing before the University of Tübingen: and it may be said of him that no man has done more to familiarise the Church of England with the vitally important developments in Biblical theology in Germany in recent times. When Barth broke like a bombshell over the sleeping tents of Anglicanism, only those who had attended Hoskyns' lectures in the old lecture-room at Corpus found little of novelty either in the idiom or in the theme. His translation of Barth's *Commentary on Romans* (1933), apart from being a very notable linguistic feat, is an historic landmark. His own reputation as a New Testament theologian stood even higher in Germany than it did at home: it was enhanced by the publication of his essay on *Jesus the Messiah* in *Mysterium Christi* (1930), a composite work arising out of the Canterbury and Eisenach (Wartburg) Conferences, and one to which German and English theologians contributed: and he had the privilege of being connected with other scholars of international distinction in the preparation of Professor Gerhard Kittel's *Theologisches Wörterbuch*. But his best known work is *The Riddle of the New Testament* (1931: 2nd edn., revised, 1936), which combines profound and incisive scholarship with a wide popular appeal, and which was written in collaboration with the Rev. F. N: Davey, a former pupil.

This outline of his major contributions to the study of theology may be supplemented by a notice of one or two of his more scattered pieces. A penny pamphlet, *Christ and Catholicism* (The Congress Books, No. 12: Society of SS. Peter and Paul, 1923), is still of interest as containing in germ much of his later thought: its immediate purpose was 'to point out that the characteristic notes of Catholic Christianity can be traced back to the teaching of our Lord Himself, and that, therefore, His Gospel was not so "simple" as is often supposed'. Its opening paragraph reads curiously to-day, and again we can measure by that sense of strangeness the significance of Hoskyns' achievement in the field of New Testament theology.

'At the present time it is widely assumed that the Christianity of the New Testament and the Catholic faith are two different systems, and that the religion taught by our Lord bears no vital relation to the Catholic religion, which claims his authority. It is said that he taught a simple religion of the love of God and the love of man, that he made no peculiar claims for his own person, that he was a Jew anxious for the purification of the religion of his people, that he was crucified because he refused to compromise with the

Jewish authorities, and that he lived and died as merely
one, though that one the greatest, of the prophets.
After his death his disciples, and St Paul in particular,
are said gradually to have deified him, invented the
Church with its doctrines and sacraments and its
emphasis on the miraculous, and elaborated (and, in
so doing, corrupted) the simplicity of his teaching.
The outcome of this development was the Catholic
religion, which dominated Western civilisation till
the Reformation, when Luther rediscovered something of the original religion, it being left for the
scholars of the nineteenth century to complete his
discovery. Now at last, it is claimed, the true Jesus of
history has been found, and we are free of dogmas,
free of the miraculous, "supernatural" additions to
genuine Christianity, free of sacramental and sacri-
ficial worship, free of the Church.'

Admittedly, the superstitions which he was then de-
nouncing—and of which a more elaborate analysis may
be found in *The Christ of the Synoptic Gospels**—do still to
some extent persist among the uninstructed. Nevertheless, no competent authority to-day would write that
paragraph precisely in those terms.

Christ and Catholicism, as will have been observed, had
something of the character of a 'Party' manifesto. But,
although he adhered, unhesitatingly and to the end, to
the Catholic side, Hoskyns was never in any danger of
becoming in any narrow sense a 'Party' man, or of
making what Bishop Creighton, with unerring judgment, regarded as the supreme mistake of Laud's career

* *Essays Catholic and Critical*, pp. 154–8.

—the mistake of fighting for great principles on small issues.* What Creighton meant was, that Laud saw that the principle of intellectual freedom in the Church of England required to be defended against Puritan intolerance, and, to that end, invoked the power of the State to compel external uniformity: in other words, that he said, in effect, 'The Puritans design to narrow the system of the Church of England: we'll fight them, and beat them, on the question of the position of the Holy Table in their churches'. The mind of Hoskyns never worked along those lines. He was not, indeed, insensitive to the exigencies of the party conflict, and certain phrases in the paper on 'The Apostolicity of the Church', which he read at the Anglo-Catholic Congress of 1930, had, and was recognised as having, a direct bearing upon a particular concrete situation.

'And now the Bishops....

'In our modern controversies we Catholics are not concerned primarily with a question of organisation. We are concerned with the nature of the Gospel, at a time when there is much vague talk about the independent motions of the Holy Spirit. Taught by the New Testament, we are bound to think of the Episcopate as preserving the witness of the Apostles, and to demand this of the Bishops. The Bishops are not mystical persons to whom we owe some strange kind of undefined mysterious obedience. The Bishops are responsible to bear witness to Jesus Christ, the Son of God, and to hold the Church to that witness. Nor does the Episcopate offer an opportunity to gifted

* *The Failure of Laud*, in *The Mind of St Peter, and other Sermons*, p. 98.

individuals to occupy an exalted position and to tyrannise over those who are endowed to a lesser degree with intellectual or other gifts. The authority of the Bishops depends solely on their link with the Apostles, though we may hope that this link may be productive of virtue and courage and of intellectual and spiritual insight. Such resultant powers are, however, wholly secondary. Nor (and I would like to emphasise this in an assembly of Catholics) do the Bishops represent the whole history of the Church and bring the whole weight of this history crashing down upon our shoulders. There is much in the history of the Church which we should do well to forget or be entirely ignorant of. The Bishops represent the history of the Church only in so far as that history has been controlled by the will of God perfected in Jesus Christ. In this sense they link the past with the creative work of God in the present and in the future.'*

But the real point about this extract is that Hoskyns was not talking about Birmingham: he was talking about Bishops, and about the significance of the Episcopate in the Church of God as declared to us by the New Testament: in a word, he was talking of the New Testament. Yet, although he was never interested in the party conflict for its own sake—'We are concerned with the nature of the Gospel'—he was the last man to regard secondary issues as irrelevant or unimportant, precisely because he saw how they contained that primary issue. Such was his theological insight that he always saw the whole within the part. But it would be utterly erroneous

* *Report of the Anglo-Catholic Congress*, 1930, pp. 88, 90.

to think of Hoskyns as a controversialist. He was not really a controversialist at all, because he was a theologian and a prophet.

'*We are concerned with the nature of the Gospel*': and in his later work he tended even more markedly to leave the 'Catholic' question to take care of itself, and to concentrate upon this fundamental problem of the nature of the Gospel, with particular attention to the problem of what it meant to the people by whom, and for whom, it was written. Of nothing was Hoskyns more intolerant than of the natural human tendency to read things into it; as, for example, modern popular humanitarian or humanistic ideas. *The Riddle of the New Testament* is the fruit of this intellectual self-discipline.

'... When the Catholic Christian kneels at the words *incarnatus est* or at the words *and was incarnate*, he marks with proper solemnity his recognition that the Christian Religion has its origin neither in general religious experience, nor in some peculiar esoteric mysticism, nor in a dogma, and he declares his faith to rest upon a particular event in history. Nor is the Catholic Christian peculiar in this concentration of faith. This is Christian Orthodoxy, both Catholic and Protestant. In consequence, the Christian Religion is not merely open to historical investigation, but demands it, and its piety depends upon it. Inadequate or false reconstruction of the history of Jesus of Nazareth cuts at the heart of Christianity. The critical and historical study of the New Testament is therefore the prime activity of the Church....'*

* *The Riddle of the New Testament*, p. 10.

As to the particular problem implicit in the title of
his earlier pamphlet, *Christ and Catholicism*, which was,
as it were, the taking-off point for his later work, it may
suffice to quote the opening sentence of his essay on *The
Christ of the Synoptic Gospels* as indicating his mature
conviction. 'For the Catholic Christian', he wrote,
'"*Quid vobis videtur de Ecclesia, What think ye of the
Church?*" is not merely as pertinent a question as "*Quid
vobis videtur de Christo, What think ye of the Christ?*": it is
but the same question differently formulated.'* The
significance of this assertion was that it cut right across
the traditional conflict between Liberal Protestantism
(Harnack) and Catholic Modernism (Loisy). To regard
Hoskyns as a great protagonist in a twentieth-century
controversy is, therefore, completely to misunderstand
him. He was a scientific student of the Bible, and it is in
that field that his importance lies. He was very reluc-
tant to press conclusions about contemporary controversies. He was clear in his own mind that his task was
to study and expound the Gospel of God as given in the
New Testament: and he was righteously incensed with
some reviewer who insisted on discussing *The Riddle of
the New Testament* in terms of 'the Battle', instead of as a
piece of scientific Biblical work. For the questions with
which he was wrestling in his writings, his lectures, his
sermons, and his supervisions—the questions which he
found to be forced upon him by the Biblical material
itself, and which he in turn forced upon the attention of
that section of the theological public which listened to
him—were not the stock controversial questions, but
rather, 'What does the fulfilment of the Old Testament

* *Essays Catholic and Critical*, p. 153.

mean?' 'What is New Testament Greek, and where does it come from?'

I am not qualified to trace the stages through which Hoskyns passed in his quest to discover what the Gospel was, and what it meant. I am therefore grateful to the Rev. J. O. Cobham, Principal of the Queen's Theological College, Birmingham, for his permission to quote from a private letter a tentative reconstruction of that progress.

'When you and I were undergraduates [after the War]', writes Mr Cobham, 'Hoskyns was seeking to expound the theology of the New Testament largely in terms of Catholic Modernism. He had, as you say, sat under Harnack at Berlin, had been influenced by Schweitzer, and was seeking to expound the New Testament in terms of Loisy and to some extent of the Religionsgeschichtlicheschule ["History of Religion" school of thought]. He was also under the influence of those who sought to find authority for Christian belief in "religious experience". The religion of the New Testament had authority because it came out of a unique religious experience—the religious experience of the primitive Church. In his lectures he began with the later books of the New Testament and worked backwards, separating the Gospels as giving the religious experience of the Church (here he used Loisy) from the Gospels as giving the authentic teaching of the Lord. And, though in theory he should have worked back to the problem of the authentic teaching of the Lord, in point of fact he hardly ever arrived there. Thus the impression was conveyed that the final authority was the religious experience of the Church. It was typical of this that in 1924 he sent me to Marburg largely to sit at the feet of Rudolf Otto and Friedrich Heiler. Yet I do not think that Hoskyns was really happy with either Rudolf Otto or Heiler. The welcoming of Barth—he read the *Römerbrief* for the first time in 1924 or 1925— was the welcoming of one who spoke of "revelation" rather than of "religious experience".

'The question of Hoskyns and Barth needs to be handled with considerable care. Hoskyns was never a Barthian. That, I am sure, wants saying. But at the time when his own work on the New Testament was forcing him away from Catholic Modernism, he discovered Barth as someone who supplied him with a language through which to express what he himself was discovering in the New Testament. And the Barth he appreciated was the Barth of the *Römerbrief*, not the Barth of the *Dogmatik....*

'Then comes the influence of Kittel and the *Wörterbuch*. That dates, I suppose, from the conferences at Canterbury and Eisenach. But I know that, when in 1930 I returned to Westcott House, and again went to Hoskyns' lectures, I found them radically different from what they had been. He was not only using the language of paradox he had learnt from Barth, but also using the lexicographical method of the *Wörterbuch*. And I think that something should be said of his recovery of the doctrine that the Greek of the New Testament is in a very significant sense "the language of the Holy Ghost"....

'The position he reached made him the severe antagonist of Liberalism in all its forms. That is why I hope that you will drop the phrase "Liberal Catholicism".

He was concerned to give Catholics a sure basis in the Gospel. But he was no less concerned to recall Evangelicals to the Gospel. That is why his lectures were so keenly attended by members of Wesley House. If Evangelicals within the Church of England were less appreciative, that was perhaps because Hoskyns was never tired of insisting that the Gospel implied the Church. But I think there is danger in stressing too much Hoskyns as an Anglo-Catholic, lest Evangelicals within the Church of England fail even now to realise that Hoskyns was for many years fighting the cause of Evangelicalism almost single-handed.'

As his fame grew, the demands upon his time and energy became more exacting. (Latterly he used some-times to question the legitimacy of those demands so lightly and even recklessly made upon the clergy, which take them careering gratuitously about the country away from their work, their parishes, even their dioceses, and often, inevitably, to the detriment of the jobs that they are being paid to do.) Everywhere he was in demand as a lecturer and as a preacher. Yet it may be admitted that, despite the perfect clarity of his exposition, those who were previously unfamiliar with the premises, the idiom, the objectives, and the natural movement of his thought, were liable to feel themselves rather beyond their depth: I doubt whether the normal under-graduate (not a theologian) during his first three academic years could really appreciate what Hoskyns was driving at, but in the fourth year, if a man stayed up for it, his sermons in the College Chapel suddenly became luminous and arresting: and I remember a course of lectures at Sion College in 1934 by which most of the older clergy, although impressed, seemed to be somewhat puzzled or bewildered, whereas the effect upon the younger men, of whom many must have sat under him as undergraduates, was indeed electrifying.

But the centre of his influence lay in Cambridge: and for the past fifteen years it was true of him, perhaps to a greater degree than of any of his colleagues or seniors in the Faculty of Divinity, that young ordinands gravitated to this University for the express purpose of studying theology under his direction. It is no dishonour to the Divinity Professors to record how men, and women, came to Cambridge for the sake of Hoskyns. He had no doubt at all that the study upon which he was engaged —'the critical and historical study of the New Testament'—was the highest task a man could face: and in his hands theology became dynamic and creative. His lectures on the Theology and Ethics of the New Testament were exceptionally vivid, forceful, trenchant, and unexpected, and were delivered with a sustained enthusiasm and excitement which it is impossible for anyone who heard them ever to forget: by contrast, his sermons, though equally emphatic, seemed curiously restrained. It was through these lectures, and through his College teaching and his supervisions, that he left his abiding mark upon the Church of England: for through them he exerted an unrivalled influence upon the younger clergy, who remain to carry on the work from which God in His inscrutable wisdom has now recalled him.

He was not a philosophic theologian, either by temperament or by training. It is, no doubt, unlikely that he would, like Barth, have denied the right of a natural theology to exist: yet it is equally improbable that he would ever have come to interest himself in the wider, if more nebulous, problems of philosophical theology, for he was essentially a New Testament scholar, and his great achievement consisted in re-anchoring Anglican theology to the Scriptures. It was upon the problems of New Testament exegesis that he concentrated his intellectual powers as a theologian: and you may generally recognise a pupil of Hoskyns by the fact that, when he says 'theology', what he means is 'New Testament theology'.

It is, however, of importance to guard against the possible impression that in his critical and historical study of the New Testament he steered an easy or an even course. To some of us who knew him over a long period, it has seemed that his work as a New Testament theologian and preacher falls into three main periods or divisions. In his first period, the whole pattern of things —the Church, the Sacraments, the Gospel, the Eschatology—was relatively neat and orderly and secure, and supplied the necessary framework of his studies. But then, as he penetrated deeper into the very heart of the New Testament problem, this neat and orderly pattern became disordered, insecure, and problematic in its outlines: he saw that the very foundations of his subject were shaken by the impact of those mysterious questionings which lie embedded even within the ultimate certainties of the Christian faith: and, precisely because he came to grips with New Testament study, he saw that New Testament study is in essence a turbulent and tempestuous thing. Inevitably, therefore, his language began to be difficult and obscure: he was to us as a man wrestling out of sight with tremendous intellectual problems which lay beyond the range of our more limited experience of the Word of God. And then, when he had, as it were, been through this solitary intellectual turmoil and had come out triumphant on the further side, and when the whole pattern and framework of his thought was once more beginning to emerge, transmuted by that struggle, but once more neat and orderly and secure: then, at that moment, came the Divine command which often seems to us so inexplicable: 'Draw out now, and bear unto the Governor of the feast.' It is not for us to penetrate into the mysteries of the Divine purpose. *The secret things belong unto the Lord our God.*

But Hoskyns' interests were in no sense purely academic. As Dr Pickthorn has observed: 'It was just because he was wholly devoted to the New Testament and to the historical study of it that almost everything human invited his comprehension.'

'...He was a very notable and noble example of integrity, of being all of a piece, of intellect and character forming each other in a virtuous circle of which the parts could not be differentiated and of which the centre was God. His mind was peculiarly simple and direct, and all his experience was real and went straight to his heart and to his head. He never forgot he was an East End child, any more than he ever forgot the ancient glories of his family, and it would be difficult to say whether it was more of an intellectual or a moral strength to him that he had an almost unique awareness of the reality of other people: he was immensely interested in the social and racial and accidental things that differentiated them, street

cleaners or farm labourers or princes or prelates, the
whole external diversity of human life, but though he
would take these things solemnly on ceremonious
occasions he never took them seriously, nor for a
moment forgot the eternal brotherhood and the
essential equality of man. He learned to know
Germany and the Germans exceptionally well, and,
for one who was naturally a south-country man with
scholarly and gentlemanly tastes, he retained from
his Sunderland and Sheffield days and from his
chaplaincy with a Lancashire Division a remarkably
intimate understanding of the north-country working
population. A man of peace and good-will if ever
there was one, and a non-combatant who recollected
in tranquillity the emotions and experiences of war
and warriors without any illusion of bitterness or of
sentimentality, Hoskyns brought all this width of
social and human perception as a matter of course
and without any self-consciousness to all his theological work however technical and to every problem
of teaching and conduct.'*

If, then, his interests in his own subject were markedly
limited to his own particular field, it would be far from
true to suggest that his interests were ever limited to his
own subject. 'He must have been one of the few theologians who read the *Farmer and Stockbreeder* most weeks,
and rarely without benefit to his Biblical studies.'† He
had a deeper understanding of the Problem of History
than most professional historians, largely, I think, as the

---

* Obituary notice, signed 'K.W.M.P.', in the *Cambridge Review*,
October 15, 1937.
   † *Ibid.*

result of his unfinished work on the Fourth Gospel: and
his discovery of the significance and intention of Archbishop Parker's collection of books and manuscripts in
the Corpus Library, of which he was Librarian, was a
notable contribution to our appreciation of the Elizabethan Settlement. Unfortunately he could never be
prevailed upon to publish his findings in any field in
which he regarded himself only as an amateur. Yet he
had an extraordinary genius, not confined to his professional studies as a theologian, for recognising and
concentrating upon the real issues. Vitality and realism
were the outstanding qualities of his thought: he had no
patience for those who attempted to evade or soften
what he called 'the roughness of the Biblical material',
or to refine it into 'a delicate spiritual piety': and I
remember him once observing in private conversation
that it was almost to be regretted that we could not
sacrifice a bull once a year, preferably on a hot day in
summer, in order to enable theological students to
understand the meaning of the word 'sacrifice' in the
Old Testament. On another occasion, in the course of
a discussion on the necessity of Greek in the Theological
Tripos, he based his argument on the fact that the
Gospels are strange to us men of the twentieth century,
and that to pass the gulf which separates us from them
is an infinitely difficult task. 'Now, learning Greek is
part of that task. The strange language is a symbol of
the strangeness of thought that must be passed through
before we can understand the Gospels aright.' Precisely
because of these continual flashes of perception, he was
a brilliant as he was also an enthusiastic conversation-
alist, and his views on topics as divergent—though he

would never have allowed that epithet—as the Theory of Cricket (he was a devotee of Lord's) and the Teaching of Scripture in Secondary Schools (he was a member of the Hadow Committee on Education) were always incisive and illuminating. His grasp of the latter of these problems was indeed remarkable, and it is vitally important that the conclusions at which he had arrived should not be disregarded now that they have lost the benefit of his reasoned but impassioned advocacy.

Hoskyns was a great teacher, perhaps one of the greatest of his time, and it is certain that his influence upon the mind and life of the Church of England has not been terminated, much less obliterated, by his death. It is indeed a tragedy that the measure of that influence and the quality of his scholarship should be so inadequately represented by the tale of his published writings. Yet the really striking thing is how much of his work had been brought to the point at which others can and will carry it on. And that is perhaps the highest praise that can be given to any teacher, particularly to one who dies, like Hoskyns, suddenly and unexpectedly. At the same time, it should be placed on record that his influence on the young men was out of all proportion to the measure in which they understood his theology. And I desire that it may be remembered that this applies not least to the writer of this memoir.

Let me, therefore, conclude by quoting once more from the obituary notice by Dr Pickthorn in the *Cambridge Review*:

'He had far too deep a heart to be a Humanitarian, and far too free a mind to be a Liberal. He was far too generous to be other-worldly. He was every inch a priest, without any pretention. In a society like the Corpus high table in the post-war years, where almost every one was young, where conversation was unrestrained and almost wholly disrespectful and frequently ribald, he always, without effort and without the least itch to correct, preserved his personal and priestly dignity; he was always intimate with every colleague, and entertained by all of them, without ever allowing it to be conceivable that his merriment had any tinge of that offence into which parsons sometimes slip when their collars are unbuttoned. Outside the lecture room and the pulpit he never tried to teach or preach, but every one of his colleagues was continually learning from him, and he learnt a good deal from them, and was always charming and magnanimous in his appreciation of their assistance.

'... He never lost touch with a person or institution he had ever known (characteristically, he had much to do with the allying of Cambridge colleges to their Oxford sisters), and the more numerous were the objects of his affection the deeper was his affection for each of them, so that in him there could be no question of competing claims between college and family, church and country, ideal aspirations and practical tasks, sociability and spirituality. Whenever he swept a room it was to the glory of the Lord, and so it was when he hit a ball or threw a fly, but he was incapable of assuming that what he wanted for the times was what the Lord had always intended.'

Hoskyns was Dean of Chapel of Corpus Christi College, Cambridge, from 1919 until his death in 1937. The sermons which are printed in this volume have been selected from those which he preached in the College Chapel during his period of office. They do not, of course, represent his final contribution to theology. Nor, on the other hand, are they intended to provide a record, or material for a record, of his theological development. They are intended only to exhibit Hoskyns as a Preacher.

The course on *Christian Eschatology* was preached during the Michaelmas and Lent Terms of the academic year 1926–7. The course on *Sin and the Remission of Sins*—perhaps the greatest course of sermons that we ever had from him—was preached during the corresponding period of the year 1927–8. Five years later (1932–3) came *The Vocabulary of the New Testament—the Language of the Church*. This is the course which superficial critics will automatically label 'Barthian period' because it contains certain of the words and phrases that are commonly associated with the theology of Karl Barth. Yet a little reflection will suggest that the influence of Kittel and the *Wörterbuch* is even more conspicuous in these pages. And it has also to be said, first, that, although Hoskyns did avail himself of some of Barth's vocabulary because he found that it expressed what he himself was trying to say, the phrases which he used were not the most characteristically Barthian: and, secondly, that nobody can be qualified to discuss the relation of Hoskyns' theology to that of Barth without having previously read and studied the open letter to Barth from Hoskyns in the

Barth *Festgabe**—a very careful piece of writing in which Hoskyns picked out what he appreciated in Barth and was silent about much else.

The course on *The Homilies* (1934–5), like the course on the Thirty-Nine Articles (not included here), is significant, not only in itself, but also as illustrating a very important side of Hoskyns' character, namely, his piety and passionate devotion towards the Church of England. This might be illustrated also from the shorter courses, of a more or less historical-biographical character (studies in life and thought), to which he used very often to devote the Easter Term. Such were the courses on Bishop Butler and on William Law. Those who were privileged to hear them will appreciate with how great hesitation and reluctance I passed them over in order to include the two sermons on *The Importance of the Parker MSS. in the College Library* (1932), mainly on the grounds that these latter constitute a contribution of primary importance to our knowledge of the Elizabethan Settlement, and one of which professional historians should no longer be deprived.

My policy as editor has been to adhere as closely as possible to the author's manuscripts, restricting my own activity to such minor duties as that of preserving some sort of consistency in capitals and punctuation. The Scriptural quotations are taken directly from the MSS.: but in regard to the quotations from the Homilies, I have ventured to use the admirable text published by the Oxford University Press in 1859, in preference to the

---

* *Theologische Aufsätze: Karl Barth zum 50. Geburtstag* (1936), pp. 525–7. Since this is not easily available to English readers, the letter will be found printed as an Appendix at the end of this book.

particular seventeenth-century edition (folio in sixes, John Norton, 1633) which happened to be used by Hoskyns. It remains only for me to express my obligation to the Editor and publisher of *Theology* for permission to use an article of mine which appeared in the September number (1937)* as the basis of this memoir, and to those of Hoskyns' old pupils and colleagues who, by their criticisms and suggestions, have enabled me to correct and supplement it.

CHARLES SMYTH

Corpus Christi College, Cambridge
  Feast of the Epiphany, 1938

---

* *In Memoriam: Canon Sir Edwyn Hoskyns. Theology*, vol. xxxv, pp. 135–41.

I

ESCHATOLOGY

(1926–27)

I

For some time now I have thought that the whole question of Christian Eschatology ought to be dealt with in this Chapel, and, with some misgiving, I propose to attempt to face the problem during these two winter terms.

There is a village in the fell country of Westmorland, not far from Shap, which lies remote from the haunts of the ordinary tourist. Had you visited it during the summer on a Sunday you would have found almost the whole population, male and female, crowding the church for the morning service—a not altogether usual sight in modern England. Curiosity, if not religious duty, might perhaps have prompted you to desire to discover what had thus moved the village people, and to enter yourself in order to satisfy your curiosity. At first there would have appeared nothing strange, just an ordinary church, just the ordinary morning service, and the quite ordinary Westmorland music. Only when the vicar commenced his sermon was the secret of the hardly suppressed excitement betrayed. With passionate conviction he declared the end of the present order to be imminent. Civilisation was tottering on the brink of destruction. No intelligent reform could save it, no social reform could postpone the disaster. The world as it is is doomed, and Armageddon is at hand. The Lord is about to appear in His wrath as the Judge and only those who are His will pass through the terror unscathed.

No doubt you would have left the church rather shocked, wondering how it is possible for an intelligent and well-bred man to express such opinions in public, and why even the inhabitants of a remote village should be so visibly affected by what he said.

Had you known something of Christian History, however, you would have remembered that periodically there has arisen in the heart of the Christian Church a vivid expectation of the End, and that not only villages but whole cities have been moved as Florence was at the preaching of Savonarola, or the West when the year 1000 drew closer and closer.

This expectation of the End is called in Christian language Eschatology, from the Greek word ἔσχατα (τὰ ἔσχατα, the Last Things). In systematic Christian Theology it forms the final chapter in Christian dogmatics, and it means no more than Christian belief about the End, without any necessary reference to its imminence. In certain forms of Christian piety, however, the supposed imminence of the End is an integral element in eschatological belief, and gives it its real significance. That is to say, it is not merely the belief that the present order will at some unknown date come to an end, which has been important for Christian experience, but the belief that the time is not far distant, and that the old order may pass away and the new order arrive at any moment.

It is with this latter form of Eschatology that I propose to deal, to discuss its place in Christian piety (understanding by Eschatology the expectation of a new order of things entering catastrophically at any moment, and felt to be at hand), and further to deal with the question of the value of such a belief and its danger.

Such questions as these are suggested by the scene in the Westmorland village, and by the reflection that the vicar may be saying something which is fundamental in the Christian religion, though he may be saying it very crudely, and may be drawing false or dangerous conclusions from his convictions.

Such questions are also suggested by the New Testament itself, but this requires proof and to this I would first direct your attention.

There is, of course, no question about the Eschatology of the Apocalypse, the Book of the Revelation. The Christian author clearly expects the great catastrophe to be about to break forth. He sees in a vision the seals opened, and the vials of the wrath of God poured out upon the earth; he hears the noise of the divine thunder, sees the stars falling and the mountains and islands moved out of their places, and the kings of the earth, the rich men and the great men hiding in the rocks of the mountains. He cries: 'The great day of the wrath of God is come, and who shall be able to stand?' (ch. vi). 'Babylon the great is fallen, is fallen.' Only the faithful Christians who have washed their robes in the blood of the Lamb, who had been persecuted but had not worshipped the great Beast, will survive the destruction which is coming.

To all this we may say, Yes, but this is a strange, isolated book in the New Testament: it is not a representative primitive Christian writing, and the Church has always found it difficult and rather unsatisfactory: it was only accepted among the authoritative Christian writings at a comparatively late date, and even then because of its supposed Apostolic authorship rather than for its intrinsic worth. All this is no doubt partially true. There is no other book in the New Testament quite like it. But this is to miss the point. The point is whether the underlying expectation of a new order imminent does not also underlie the other New Testament writings.

We cannot, indeed, get rid of the New Testament Eschatology by sacrificing the Apocalypse.

St Paul's epistles are full of it, especially his earlier epistles. In one passage in his First Epistle to the Thessalonians he summarises the Gospel as follows. He reminds his converts how they 'turned from idols to serve the living and true God and to wait for his Son from heaven whom he raised from the dead, even Jesus, who delivered us from the wrath to come' (I Thessalonians i. 9, 10). That is, the Christian converts are men and women who have turned from heathenism, and worship the living God; after this conversion they await the coming or Advent of His Son to judge sinners and to deliver from an evil world those who have been saved from the Wrath—namely, the Christians.

In another passage towards the end of the Epistle to the Romans he writes: 'It is high time to awake out of sleep, for now is our salvation nearer than when we believed; the night is far spent, the day is at hand: let us therefore cast off the works of darkness, and let us put on the armour of light: let us walk...not in chambering and wantonness, not in strife and envy' (Romans xiii. 11 ff.). St Paul's moral appeal is there based on the belief that the Day is breaking and only the righteous man will or can share in its glory.

To St Paul, the whole world is passing to destruction, and the Wrath of God hangs like the sword of Damocles over it. He restlessly passes from city to city, convinced that only by conversion to Christianity can men be saved from the Wrath to come. The Christian mission is urgent largely because there is so little time. He writes: 'The wrath of God is being revealed against all unrighteousness of men' (Romans i. 18). 'God commendeth his love towards us, in that while we were yet sinners Christ died for us. Much more then, being now justified by his blood, shall we be saved from the wrath through him' (Romans v. 8 f.).

In another passage he explains the ground of his almost ferocious attack on the Jews who persecute the Christians. 'The Jews', he says, 'forbade us to speak to the Gentiles that they might be saved, even though the wrath is now breaking out upon them' (I Thessalonians ii. 16), or again: 'The preaching of the cross is foolishness to them who are passing to destruction, but to us who have been saved it is the power of God' (I Corinthians i. 18). There is the contrast—the unbelieving world ripe for destruction—the converted Christians, however, within the sphere of the mercy of God.

Nor are these isolated or unimportant passages. Such a belief underlies almost every word we have of St Paul's writings. He is not concerned to Christianise a civilisation, to remove slavery or to abolish war, to purify statecraft or to polish education. He is simply concerned to save men from the damnation which threatens them. Nor does he foresee a long Christian history expanding before him. There is but a little time and then the Lord will come. The only question which really matters is that every man must stand before the Judgment seat of God, and how will he then appear?

Marriage, what is the use of it? Possessions, land, property, what do they avail? 'This I say, brethren', he writes to the Corinthians (I Corinthians vii. 29 ff.), 'the time is short: it remaineth that they that have wives be as though they had none, and they that buy as though they possessed not. For the fashion of this world is passing away.'

And so we might proceed through the Pauline Epistles, and the question becomes pressing. Is our old Westmorland vicar after all so ridiculous, so unchristian? Is it not possible that it is we who are reading our New Testament with our eyes blindfolded, picking out the things which appeal to us, and which support our serene tranquillity, and our modern philanthropy and good-humoured reforms?

Is Christianity after all so friendly and this-worldly a religion as we have thought it? Is it not perhaps uneasy, dangerous, crude, springing from a sense of utter insecurity, and thus less easily harmonised with our modern ideas than we have imagined?

Yes, but, someone answers, you are misunderstanding the nature of the Christian religion. Paulinism is not Christianity. St Paul, say learned and pious men, complicated Christianity, turned it into a theology, encumbered it with impossible accretions, damaged its simplicity, and at last we are recovering from his teaching and pushing behind it to the real essence of the Christian religion. Christianity is the teaching of Christ, and to be a Christian is to follow Him.

Well, let us accept the challenge, and see if we can escape the problem by piercing behind St Paul to our Lord Jesus Christ. We have our Gospels, and, at least

in the first three, we have the record of His teaching;
the documents are there for us to read. What then was
the Gospel of Jesus—the good news which He brought
and for which He died? Next Sunday I propose to face
this question, at least in outline.

But before leaving the Eschatology of St Paul, there
is one thing which we must not forget. It is common in
certain quarters nowadays to pass lightly over St Paul.
But we should remember that after all it seems to have
been the Christianity of St Paul which did in fact
convert men and women. He did bring men to God by
his Gospel, and through his agency men and women
were purified and transformed.

If therefore it were found that the teaching of Jesus
and that of St Paul moved on two different planes, we
have still not thereby done with St Paul. An even
greater problem would then have to be faced.

II

Last Sunday I endeavoured to shew that St Paul's life
and work and writings are largely unintelligible unless
we assume that he believed that the end of the present
order was at hand and that the Wrath of God was about
to break forth. The intensity of his missionary activity
largely depended upon this belief; men and women
were going to destruction, and conversion to Christianity
was the only means of salvation from the Wrath of God.
The time was short.

Upon this belief also the peculiar vigour and radical-
ism of St Paul's moral demands were largely grounded.
Men were about to stand before the Judgment seat of

God or to appear in the Presence of the Christ, and nothing could save them but that righteousness which springs from a radical moral change of heart, attainable only by faith in the power of God revealed through Christ and actively at work in the communities of Christians.

By their works men would be judged. There was no escape from the righteousness of God. No magic would save them, no membership in a nation however august —to be a Jew availeth nothing. There was but one means of salvation—the actual possession of that righteousness which is of faith.

Hence all these moral problems which arise when human society and human civilisation are felt to be more or less stable—the proper use of wealth, the care of property, the duties of citizenship, the education of children—meant little or nothing to him. Such questions were blotted out, and his mind was controlled by the thought of the Advent of the Christ and the condition in which men would find themselves when they appeared in His Presence. In other words, Eschatology, or the belief that the new and final order of things was about to break forth, spurred on the great missionary, and largely explains the passionate earnestness of the letters he wrote to those who had been recently converted.

The question which now arises is the relation of the Gospel preached by St Paul to the Gospel of Jesus. Was that, too, eschatological? It is to this problem that I wish to direct your attention.

All the Evangelists agree that the preaching of John the Baptist provided the immediate background of our

Lord's public ministry, and that in a very real sense the Lord continued his work. Now the most ancient Christian tradition concerning John, which is embodied in the first three Gospels, is that John was a pure eschatological preacher. He drew the crowds out into the desert with the cry 'Repent, the kingdom of heaven is at hand', and his words to the Pharisees and Sadducees make perfectly clear what he meant: 'Ye offspring of vipers, who warned you to flee from the wrath which is coming?' 'The axe is laid to the root of the tree, every tree therefore that bringeth not forth good fruit is hewn down and cast into the fire.' The New Order and the destructive Wrath of God are about to appear. Only a radical change can save men from the Wrath.

The baptism of John was an eschatological baptism. He baptised the crowds into repentance and remission of sins in order that they might be prepared for the coming of the Lord, and bring forth fruits worthy of the repentance.

He felt himself to be the Herald of the Messiah, and His immediate predecessor. 'He that cometh after me is mightier than I, whose shoes I am not worthy to bear. He shall baptise you with the Holy Ghost and with fire' (that is, He will bring in the New Order of Spirit-filled men and women), 'whose fan is in his hand, and he will throughly cleanse his threshing floor and he will gather his wheat into the garner but the chaff he will burn up with unquenchable fire'—that is, with the coming of the Messiah the Judgment will be set.

From this scene emerges the life and death of Jesus. The Lord opens His teaching by repeating and endorsing the words of the Baptist, 'Repent ye, for the kingdom of

heaven is at hand.' And, moreover, our Lord endorses
not only John's preaching, but also his interpretation of
his person. He was the Elijah of the prophecy of
Malachi, who would appear before the Day of the Lord.
'Behold, I will send you Elijah the prophet before the
great and terrible day of the Lord.' This prophecy is
picked up and applied to John by our Lord. 'What
went ye out for to see? a prophet? Yea, I say unto you
and much more than a prophet. This is he of whom it is
written, Behold, I send my messenger before thy face,
who shall prepare thy way before thee' (St Luke vii.
24 ff.). 'This is the Elijah which should come. He that
hath ears to hear, let him hear.' It seems therefore
impossible to avoid the conclusion that our Lord's
public ministry began in an eschatological atmosphere,
and that He recognised this, and gave it His approval
and sanction.

If we turn to the concluding incidents of the evangelical history, two incidents in the Passion narrative
are clearly regarded as of first-rate importance for the
interpretation of the significance of the Crucifixion and
of our Lord's Person: His words to His disciples at the
Last Supper, and the words addressed to the High
Priest with which He broke His silence during the trial
before the Sanhedrin.

The two incidents follow close upon one another, and
upon their interpretation depends our understanding of
our Lord's explanation of His death.

During the Last Supper He took bread, blessed it and
gave to the disciples, saying 'This is my Body', and He
took a cup, and gave thanks, and they all drank of it.

Then follow the explanatory and declaratory words. 'This is my Blood of the New Covenant, which is being shed for many', or, in their Matthaean form, 'This is my Blood of the New Covenant, which is being shed for many unto the remission of sins'.

Now whatever further implications there may be in our Lord's acts and words at the Supper, their primary meaning is surely plain. They are a solemn and formal declaration that His death will bring into being the New Order or New Covenant, in fact, the Kingdom of God, and the characteristic feature of the New Order is stated to be that change of heart which carries with it remission of sins.

Then follows the saying, 'But I say unto you: I will not drink henceforth of this fruit of the vine until I drink it new'—Matthew adds 'with you'—'in the Kingdom of God'.

These last words are, as they stand, pure eschatology. The imagery of the great Messianic Banquet which follows the Judgment formed an integral element in traditional Jewish eschatological language, and our Lord at this moment picks up the old language and uses it without, so far as we can see, any criticism or modification. His death will usher in the New Order, and His disciples will share in the great heavenly Banquet which follows the destruction of the powers of evil.

Further, it should be noted that the whole descriptive passage is prefaced by the saying, 'The Son of man goeth as it has been written of him', that is, written or prophesied in the Old Testament. To our Lord, therefore, His death was the climax of the divine plan for the salvation of men and for the advent of the Kingdom of God.

Then follow in quick succession the narrative of the prayer in Gethsemane and the arrest, which leads to the careful record of the trial before Caiaphas. At the trial our Lord is silent—the silence of the lamb in Isaiah's picture of the suffering Servant of God—until the High Priest asks Him the direct question, on His answer to which His condemnation must depend, since the witnesses have disagreed. 'And the high priest stood up in the midst and asked Jesus, saying: Answerest thou nothing? What is it which these witness against thee? But he held his peace and answered nothing. Again the high priest asked him and said unto him, Art thou the Christ, the Son of the Blessed? And Jesus said, I am: and ye shall see the Son of man, sitting at the right hand of power and coming with the clouds of heaven. And the high priest rent his clothes, and saith, What further need have we of witnesses, ye have heard the blasphemy: what think ye? And they all condemned him to be worthy of death.'

Here again at this supreme moment, as at the Last Supper, our Lord falls back on pure eschatology. His words are not merely an echo but a direct quotation of the passage in the Book of Daniel, where the prophet sees in a vision the end of the great kingdoms of the world symbolised under the four beasts coming out of the sea, and the Judgment is set and their authority is taken from them, and 'behold, there came with the clouds of heaven one like unto a Son of man, and unto him was given dominion and glory and a kingdom. And his dominion is an everlasting dominion which shall not pass away.'

Thus the prophet saw the vision of the Judgment and the coming of the eternal Messianic Kingdom of God.

To this prophecy our Lord points in His answer to the High Priest, and asserts that it is about to be fulfilled.

During His Passion, therefore, our Lord combines the suffering Servant of Isaiah with the glorious advent of the Kingdom and the appearance on the clouds of the Messiah, and interprets His own life and death as the fulfilment of the former, whilst the fulfilment of the latter will take place not only after His death but as a result of it. His death will usher in the New Order, 'and ye shall see the Son of man coming on the clouds of heaven with power and great glory'.

Thus the record of the opening scene of our Lord's ministry and the great utterances during the Passion betray unobscured eschatology. The evangelists shew no desire of concealing it, and to them it was clearly of the most intense significance.

In the next sermon I shall attempt to deal in outline with some salient features of our Lord's teaching, in order to discern whether elsewhere in the Gospel narratives eschatological beliefs are present or implied.

III

The conclusion reached at the end of the last sermon was that our Lord's public ministry opened and closed in an eschatological atmosphere; that is, with a vivid expectation that a wholly new order was about to appear and that the outbreak of the eternal rule of God was imminent. The Baptist's preaching, as recorded in the Synoptic Gospels, was eschatological in the sense that he proclaimed the Judgment to be at hand and that his baptism for the remission of sins was the sacramental preparation of the people to receive the coming Messiah. With this eschatological movement in Judaism our Lord associated Himself, and His first preaching was a repetition of the Gospel of John—'The kingdom of God is at hand.' Nor do the great sayings during the Passion shew any change of background, except that they express the conviction that His death is the divinely appointed means by which the New Order or Covenant or Kingdom is to be ushered in and established. The words at the Last Supper, 'I will not drink henceforth of the fruit of this vine until that day when I drink it new with you in my Father's kingdom', and the words with which He broke His silence before Caiaphas and the Sanhedrin, 'Henceforth ye shall see the Son of man sitting at the right hand of power and coming on the clouds of heaven', can mean nothing else but that He submitted to the Passion because He believed that His death stood midway between the Old and the New Order.

If this interpretation be correct, it remains to discover whether our Lord's teaching *as a whole* was or was not constructed on an eschatological foundation.

I propose to take at this point two familiar passages in the Gospels and to ask whether the usual interpretation of them is satisfactory—the Beatitudes and the Lord's Prayer. They are peculiarly important passages in the Gospels, not merely because they are so well-known, but because no reasonable critical examination can throw doubt on their authenticity. They belong to the Lost Document which both the author of our First Gospel and the author of our Third Gospel incorporate into their narratives, combining it with St Mark's Gospel. The structure of the First and Third Gospels is mainly Mark and material from this Lost Document. The Lost Document, therefore, is older than the so-called Gospel of St Matthew, older than St Luke's Gospel and perhaps older than St Mark's Gospel. Further, there is some reason to think that the tradition that the Apostle Matthew collected the Sayings of Jesus and wrote them down was originally a tradition refer-ring to this Lost Document (since it must have consisted mainly of the Lord's sayings), and that the tradition was later erroneously transferred to our First Gospel when the original Apostolic document had disappeared. If so, it is not unreasonable to suppose that the Beatitudes and the Lord's Prayer were committed to writing by the Apostle St Matthew. At any rate, we can confidently treat them as our Lord's actual words, though of course translated into Greek.

If we read through the Beatitudes, we notice at once that they emphasise a contrast between the present and the future. The gentle, the peacemakers, the mourners, the merciful, the pure in heart, and those who long for righteousness, are declared to be blessed, not because they do now possess the earth, or are the sons of God, or are comforted, or see God, or are filled with righteous-ness, but because all these things will be theirs in the future. Our Lord is here drawing in bold outlines the lineaments of those to whom the future belongs. The Kingdom when it comes belongs not to the proud and hard-hearted; not to those to whom the world as it is is wholly satisfactory; not to those who have no horror of the power of evil; not to those for whom strife and war are the bread of life. The Kingdom of God will be recruited from those who feel human society to be out of gear, and who long for a great divine intervention which will establish a new order. Such men and women, persecuted for righteousness now, are, for our Lord, destined to be the children of the Kingdom, the true sons of God, who will be filled and satisfied only when the Kingdom comes.

The last Beatitude passes from the general to the particular, and is an exhortation to the disciples of the Lord; great will be their reward in heaven, in spite of their present persecution because they are His disciples.

The first Beatitude must therefore be interpreted in the light of the others. 'Blessed are the poor, for theirs is the kingdom of God' cannot mean in its context that the oppressed possess the Kingdom now because they are poor. It must mean that those who now are conscious of oppression need not despair, since the future belongs to them and not to their oppressors.

It is almost impossible to understand these sayings except on an eschatological background. Our Lord's words lose all their vigour and point if they were not spoken as a gospel or good news to the oppressed. The New Order is about to break forth and the Kingdom is imminent. There is no suggestion that our Lord intended His hearers to understand that their *death* would be their redemption from suffering, or that the Kingdom would belong to their descendants. No, He exhorts them to stand firm and not to be overwhelmed by the present tyranny and the sorrow it brings with it, because the time of their tribulation is felt to be short.

If we turn from the Beatitudes to the Lord's Prayer, it is at once clear that both emerge from a common background. In St Matthew's Gospel, the Lord's Prayer forms a part of the Sermon on the Mount, and it is contrasted with the prayers of the Pharisees as true prayer to false. In St Luke's Gospel it follows a description of the Lord Himself praying: 'when he ceased, one of his disciples said, Lord, teach us to pray as John taught his disciples. And Jesus said to them, Whenever ye pray, say: Father, Hallowed be thy name, Thy kingdom come.'

The prayer which our Lord gave His disciples is, with the exception of one petition, simply an earnest request to God that the Kingdom may not be delayed, and that His disciples may be ready when the Kingdom appears.

The first clauses in the version in St Matthew's Gospel are variants upon the clause 'Thy kingdom come'. The petitions that God's Name may be hallowed and that His Will may be done on earth as it is in heaven define the nature of the Kingdom. It will be the time when the power of God is recognised and His Will is done.

The final petitions are prayers that the Lord's disciples may be men who can share in the Kingdom when it comes: cleansed men, whose sins have been forgiven, and who by the mercy of God have been delivered from the power of the Evil One ('forgive us our trespasses, deliver us from the Evil One'), since only the righteous can share in the Kingdom of God.

Thus far all is comparatively simple. The Lord

teaches His disciples that only one prayer is really necessary, the prayer that God may act soon, and that they may be righteous men.

But between the two sections of the prayer is inserted the petition for sufficient food. We are generally told that this shews our Lord's care for the bodily needs of His disciples, and His trust that His Father will give the disciples all that they require. Now of course this may be so. But the clause is difficult: partly because it is so different from the other petitions, partly because the actual meaning of the Greek is obscure.

The Matthaean form of the petition means literally 'give us to-day the bread for to-morrow'. St Luke has felt the difficulty and paraphrased it—'Give us each day the bread for to-morrow.' Luke's meaning is quite clear. God is asked that each day we may have sufficient food to carry us over the following day. But what did St Matthew mean—or what did the words mean in the Lost Document—and what did they mean to our Lord?

I cannot resist submitting to you an interpretation suggested last year by a very learned Jew, Dr Eisler.

He pointed out that in contemporary Judaism, that is, in the first century, the Sabbath Day was regarded as the type and symbol of the Golden or Messianic Age, in fact, of the rest and peace of the Kingdom of God which would one day come. Then he proved that to the Jews the story of the giving of the manna to the children of Israel in the desert was treated as an eschatological parable, a foreshadowing of the food of God, which would descend upon the desert of the world in the last days. Now comes the important point. In the original story of the giving of the manna, on the day before the

Sabbath a double portion of manna was gathered, that is to say, on the Friday they gathered the morrow's bread. We have now in our hands a key to the difficult petition in the Lord's Prayer. Assuming then this eschatological interpretation of the manna story to have been familiar to Jews, the petition in the Lord's Prayer becomes at once intelligible. Give us to-day the Sabbath bread, as an earnest of the imminent advent of the rule of God. The whole prayer is then of one piece, a prayer that the Kingdom may not be delayed, and the difficult Greek word—'to-morrow's bread'—has an intelligible meaning. Further, we must not forget that our New Testament is rooted in the Old Testament, and that many of the sayings are like the visible part of an ice-berg. They emerge from a submerged mass which is invisible; the part invisible to us is the contemporary interpretation of the Old Testament, or our Lord's own Old Testament allusions. Therefore, such an exegesis as that of Dr Eisler is not as isolated and fantastic as it may at first sight appear.

I do not, however, wish to tie myself to an acceptance of this particular interpretation, because the eschato-logical background of our Lord's teaching is otherwise established, at least it seems an unavoidable conclusion from our Gospel narratives.

If, then, the Beatitudes and the Lord's Prayer be proved to be eschatological utterances, and if the Baptist's preaching and the words of the Last Supper be intelligible only on an eschatological background, I need not spend more time in pointing out that the parables of the mustard seed and the leaven express the Lord's belief that a miraculously quick growth is imminent—the advent of the Kingdom: nor will it surprise us that He urges His disciples to watch, for they 'know not when the Lord of the house cometh, whether at even or at midnight or at cockcrowing or in the morning; lest coming suddenly he find them sleeping. And what I say unto you I say unto all, Watch.' Nor have we any right to declare unauthentic His words 'Verily, I say unto you, This generation shall not pass away until all these things be accomplished'.

It remains, then, to discuss the significance of such language, and its value for us. The alternatives are clear. Either such language belongs entirely to a past age, and, if so, our Lord's figure belongs to the past which is irretrievably gone, or else permanent truth is being revealed to us in such language, and we discard the eschatology and pass it by at our own peril.

The significance of our Lord's eschatology gives me my subject for next term.

IV

Last term I endeavoured to lay out before you one of the most difficult and pressing problems with which we are confronted as Christians.

On the assumption that the New Testament and our Lord's teaching and life are an authoritative expression of truth for all those who call themselves Christians, we cannot avoid the plain fact that the first Christians did both long for the End of the present order of things and expect the End to be imminent; and further that this expectation had the sanction of our Lord's own teaching. To use the technical term, Primitive Christianity was an 'eschatological' Religion: that is to say, Christian piety was largely controlled by the belief that the End of all things—the Last Things—was at hand.

Since there is no justification for the view that this represented a complete misunderstanding of our Lord's teaching, we Christians have boldly to face a very awkward problem.

Nor can we be content to leave it merely to the historians and professed theologians, since the New Testament is the standard and guide of our devotional life, and Jesus Christ is not merely sentimentally, but in very truth, our Lord. Any serious break therefore in our confidence either in our Lord's insight into truth or in the general rightness of the piety of His immediate disciples tends to damage, however subtly, the authority of the Christian religion.

What then are we to make of the eschatology? Or, to put it concretely, what are we to make of such a saying as 'Verily, I say unto you, This generation shall not pass away until all these things be accomplished'?

The answer which intelligent unbelievers give to this question is that we can make nothing of it. Jesus and His disciples belonged to a world which is irretrievably gone; they were fanatics who believed in a catastrophic end of the world, which was about to take place. Their belief was heroic, but false, and therefore they are interesting figures in history, but no more, and the modern world must therefore either discard Christianity, or rebuild it on a new foundation.

On the other hand, the answer which many earnest and intelligent Christians give to the problem is that the eschatological language is a means of expressing pictorially moral and religious truth, but that it corresponds to no historical truth. The End did not come, but the language, taken as imagery, is valuable and important religious imagery.

We are thus left on the horns of a dilemma: either our Lord's teaching and large sections of the New Testament are dangerously misleading, or they are historically untrue but pictorially or symbolically true.

I wish to prove that this statement of the dilemma presents us with a false alternative and substitutes a simple issue for what is much more complicated, and consequently ends by abstracting the Christian religion from history and reality to such an extent as to make its true nature unintelligible.

Now the ultimate question to which I am anxious to find an answer is, What is the meaning of eschatology for us as modern Christians? But there is a previous question which must be first asked and answered. What did the primitive Christians themselves make of the eschatological beliefs which formed so important an element in the teaching by which they had been converted? After all, St Paul, St John, the authors of the Acts of the Apostles, of the Epistle to the Hebrews, of the Epistles of Peter, were not men of so limited an intelligence that we are justified in assuming that they continued to use language which was meaningless when the End did not come. They had clearly found a meaning in our Lord's teaching, even though the world continued to exist. Well, then, what was this meaning? It is no good saying that they were ignorant men, they clearly were not; nor that they were symbolists in the modern

sense of the word—that is unduly to modernise St Paul
and St John. There is something in their experience
which has as yet escaped us.

I must, therefore, ask you to consider certain passages
in the New Testament which become important at this
point.

There is a difficult passage in the Second Epistle of
St Paul to the Corinthians which will repay careful
attention. It occurs in the third chapter, where he is
arguing against the old Jewish religion and comparing
it with Christianity. He takes as his starting-point the
story in the Book of Exodus of the giving of the Law to
Moses. He points out that the Law of God was written
on two stone tables, that the Jews never obeyed the
Law, and that they were all of them, therefore, unrighteous, clearly, patently, obviously unrighteous;
Jewish history was simply a history of continuous disobedience and unrighteousness. Of course, writes St
Paul. If you look at the old story you will see why.
Moses had to cover his face with a veil when he spoke
to the people, for two reasons: first, because they could
not bear to see the glory of God face to face; and secondly,
because even the vision of Moses was but fleeting and
temporary, and the illumination which that vision had
given him grew gradually dimmer and dimmer. Therefore he covered his face, lest the people might see the
glory disappearing. Then St Paul jumps. Yes, he says,
so it is with the greatest of all non-Christian religions.
The glory of God is unseen, unapproachable, dying,
dimmed. The veil lies on the hearts of men, and they
have no certain knowledge of God or access to Him. At
best the commands of God are written with ink, external

merely, and consequently knowledge is incomplete and righteousness imperfect, or actually non-existent.

This vigorous criticism of Judaism and consequently of Paganism is not the product of a dreamy idealism. St Paul is not contrasting the Jewish religion with a religion of the future or with an imaginary world of his own dreams. His language is quite clear and precise. Judaism has been fulfilled and superseded by a real faith and experience, a religion of flesh and blood. What had been written previously in ink on stone tables is now indelibly inscribed on the hearts of men and women; what had been a fleeting, transient vision of the glory of God is now a true and permanent knowledge seen 'in the face of Christ Jesus'. The veil of ignorance has been torn from the hearts of men, and men have access to God through Christ Jesus and through the preaching of the Gospel of life; the glory of this revelation of God is permanent, eternal, progressive. It is from 'glory to glory', not from light to a dim darkness.

And, further, there is to him an unanswerable proof that the new, long-desired salvation has actually arrived. The Christian knowledge of God in the face of Christ Jesus is productive of righteousness. The faithful converts are righteous men, they have passed from death to life, they are the holy people of God, saints, chosen men, blameless; in fact, as he says, the New Creation.

Christianity is the religion of the Spirit of God actually operative, transforming men and women into the likeness or image of the Son of God. Nothing comparable has been known or seen before; it is the New Order, the New Age, the New Covenant, foretold, dimly foretold perhaps, but yet foreseen by the great prophets of Israel. Hence the contrasts with which St Paul loves to play, letter—spirit, death—life, darkness—light, sin —righteousness, law—grace, and so on.

These are, no doubt, lyrical passages, but they are in praise of what is staggeringly real and concrete to him. Do not for one moment imagine that he is merely singing a rhapsody on the peculiar theme of his own spiritual or mystical experience. His own conversion is to him but one illustration among many of the advent of the New Order.

Christianity is, therefore, to St Paul, the great creative act of the mercy of God, and to be a Christian is to enter within the supernatural heavenly order, now, as it were, descending upon earth, and taking hold of flesh and blood and filling them with spiritual power. Christianity is the concretion in a living human organism of the 'Grace of the Lord Jesus Christ and the Love of God and the Fellowship of the Holy Ghost'.

Now comes the point. What is happening in all this— happening before our eyes as we read these and like passages in St Paul's epistles—happening without St Paul being altogether conscious of what he is doing?

He is using eschatological language to describe a present and concrete experience. The stars do not fall, nor do the mountains crumble away, the sun still shines and the stars continue to twinkle. The physical structure of the universe remains, but the dream of the righteousness and peace and holiness and knowledge which hitherto belonged to the eschatological hope, has become a concrete reality, and the Christians stand within this New Order of the Spirit, and the two worlds of the flesh and of the Spirit, of this world and the world beyond, become not two periods of human history but one sacramental, mystical, living whole; and the glory of God is displayed less in some hoped-for catastrophic contortion of the physical world than in the simplicity and purity of the humblest Christian convert. After all, to St Paul this last is the greatest of God's miraculous acts.

Next Sunday I must ask you to consider whether this fulfilled eschatology is merely a Pauline idea, or whether it was forced upon other Christians by the nature of Christian experience.

V

The word Eschatology means the expectation that the End of the world or of the present order is imminent. It is a woeful misunderstanding of the Christian religion to find in it merely an unsatisfied longing for a future catastrophe in which the world as we know it will suddenly come to an end, and a totally new order come into being. To be a Christian is, rather, the recognition that the great catastrophe lies in the past, that God has acted and is acting energetically, that righteousness has been attained by men and women and is attainable by us through the grace of God; that the divisions of sex and race and class are surmounted and overcome in the great catholic fellowship of men and women, Greek and barbarian, Jew and Gentile, bond and free; that God has ceased to be unknown and unrecognised, energetic in Heaven, but inactive in the affairs of men; rather His word 'is nigh thee in thy mouth and in thy heart', since we have 'the knowledge of the glory of

God in the face of Christ Jesus'. The Ecclesia of God, the Church of Christ, stands in the world as the home of salvation, because within it God is actively at work: it is the sphere of His authority, the realm of His Spirit, the Body of His Son. Salvation from sin, from pessimism, from the sense that all things pass to inevitable destruction, from materialism, is not for us Christians to be attained by dreaming of a world beyond this world, or by believing in some imminent catastrophe, but by plunging head first into Christian faith and fellowship, believing that the Ecclesia of God is the visible expression in the world of His love and His mercy.

This is Christian language: it is lyrical, it is poetic, but it is not for that reason unreal: it is rather the song of the Christian religion, the song of experienced salvation from the corruption which surrounds us.

The greatness of St Paul lay largely in the clarity of his insight into the significance of the Christian religion, and of the little groups of converted men and women, scattered about in the great cities of the Empire: and consequently, though hardly realising precisely what he was doing, he transferred the language hitherto used to describe what would follow the End of the world in order to describe the fruits of the Spirit actually being given by God to the faithful Christians.

For St Paul the New Age had come; it was a New Creation, and Christianity was the goal of history and the fulfilment of the promises of God. The Church was heaven upon earth, and the fulfilment of the eschatological hope, the hope, that is, that the Last Things were at hand. All the merely physical accompaniments of the traditional imagery of the End of the world tend to drop into the background, the stars do not fall from heaven, but goodness, self-discipline, charity, peace have in very truth dropped from heaven as the gifts of the mercy of God. Listen to St Paul's outburst at the conclusion of the eighth chapter of the Epistle to the Romans:

'Nay, in all things we are more than conquerors through him that loved us. For I am persuaded that neither death, nor life, nor angels, nor principalities, nor things present, nor things to come, nor powers, nor height, nor depth, nor any other creature, shall be able to separate us from the love of God which is in Jesus Christ our Lord.'

I must now endeavour to indicate quite shortly that this is not merely an idiosyncrasy of St Paul, but that as the years passed and the end of the world did not come our religion survived the disappointment, which was felt in many quarters, because it was primarily a possession and only secondarily a hope, and that this was understood by others as well as by St Paul.

There are two pieces of literature which have been incorporated into our New Testament, both of which, I would venture to suggest, come from the very end of the first century, if not from the beginning of the second century; the Lukan writings, i.e., the Third Gospel and the Acts of the Apostles, and the Johannine writings, the Fourth Gospel and the three Epistles.

Now, what is really remarkable about this whole later Christian literature is that the expectation of the end of the world has almost entirely fallen into the background. Not because it is an awkward bit of Christian tradition, which they simply leave out of their record, but because both St Luke and St John are confident that they understand it, and are able to interpret it.

There is a very important passage in the Acts of the Apostles which illustrates this. St Luke is looking back over the history of the past seventy years and drawing the attention of his readers to the meaning of that history. When he comes to record the beginning of the Church, he singles out the occasion when the Apostles first received the Spirit, as the birthday of the Ecclesia of God. Then comes what is surely a most amazing passage. He goes out of his way to unearth the most crudely eschatological passage from the Book of Joel. 'In the last days, saith God, I will pour forth of my spirit upon all flesh...and I will shew wonders in the heaven above, and signs on the earth beneath, the sun shall be turned into darkness, and the moon into blood.' That is Joel. Then St Luke comments that the gift of the Spirit to the Apostles was the fulfilment of the Joel passage. In other words, the coming of the Spirit is the true eschatology, the End, the New Order of God. And all converts since Pentecost consequently stand within the Kingdom of God.

With the composition of the Johannine writings the Christian religion may be said to have found its feet, and to be ready prepared for its battle with the 'world', and the writer was in a position to contemplate a history of Christianity unfolding in the future, though he never quite actually does so. To St John, Christianity is eternal life here and now; baptism and conversion are rebirth from above, they are the entrance into the Kingdom of God. Christian worship is the true and spiritual worship of God, and Christian knowledge is the knowledge of God. He who has seen the Christ and accepted Him has seen the Father. This is the Christianity of the Johannine writings. The eschatological sayings of Jesus, which in the earlier Gospels appeared to contemplate the end of the world, are transformed into the prophecies of the coming of the Spirit, which is to follow His Death and Resurrection.

'I have come', says our Lord in the Fourth Gospel, 'that ye might have life, and might have it more abundantly.' 'I am the resurrection and the life.' Hence Christianity is simply equivalent to Life and Truth.

Here we have the great triumph of primitive Christian thought: a triumph which was the result of reflection upon the words of Jesus in the light of Christian experience, a triumph which transformed Christianity from a small company of men and women who expected the end of the world to come at any minute, into the great catholic religion of men and women who had found God, and in so doing had entered into the sphere of Righteousness and Truth.

Is this Pauline, Lukan, Johannine interpretation of our Lord's teaching really justifiable? Was this triumph of Christian thought, which opened up the possibility of a history for the Christian religion, a triumph at the expense of our Lord's plain teaching? Is His language about the End and about the Kingdom of God capable of such an interpretation?

There can, I venture to suggest to you, be no real doubt as to our answer. Our Lord's eschatological language, as indeed all His teaching and actions, was mainly symbolical. To speak humanly, He felt Himself standing on the brink of a new spiritual order, an order which was to come into being as a direct result of His life and death, and which was to be the fulfilment of the longings of the greatest of the Jewish prophets. To express this Gospel He used the traditional language of Jewish expectation of the End, since it provided Him with a vehicle to express the significance of His life and death.

Had no new order actually come into being, our Lord would stand merely as a great heroic and visionary figure in history, but we are not called upon to face so negative a conclusion.

The emerging in history of the Christian Ecclesia throws a flood of light on our Lord's teaching and especially upon the eschatological element in it. We have no right to detach our Lord's life and death from the religion which took its rise from Him: they react upon each other, and a true understanding of the Christian religion involves the interpretation of our Lord's teaching and Person in the light of the spiritual experience of those who have accepted Him as Lord and Master.

I have hitherto tried to shew that the Kingdom of God on earth, and the Church of God which is faith and joy and love as an organism, is the fulfilment of our Lord's language concerning the coming of the End. But this does not wholly explain His words, nor indeed does it wholly do justice to the eschatological language which after all still remains an element in our Christian vocabulary.

VI

The Christian Religion is, then, the achievement of the Holy Spirit of God—a New Order and a New Creation. Belonging to this world, though not of this world, it wages a ceaseless warfare against both the dreamers and the cynics, against those who dream of a spiritual order which cannot be realised in the flesh and blood of our ordinary human life, and against those who float disconsolate and hopeless down the stream of human existence, crushed by its inadequacy and cynical even of its noblest aspirations.

The Church of God in the world is the expression of the powerful Wisdom of God in flesh and blood, in time and space. Only when this had been clearly understood did Christian faith emerge as the Catholic Religion for all humanity; nay more, only when such insight had been attained did the primitive Church attain an adequate understanding of the life and death of Jesus Christ, and give His vigorous imagery its veritable content. The effective energy of the Spirit of God enabled the faithful to discover heaven upon earth and thus in large measure to transform and reinterpret the eschatological beliefs of the earliest Christians.

It is now possible for us to return to the Westmorland vicar whose explosions were the immediate cause of this long series of addresses on Christian Eschatology. His reawakening of the excitement, fanned by a belief that the end of the world is at hand, is based on a radical misconception of the nature of the Christian religion. The function of a parish priest is to proclaim the Gospel, and the Gospel is quite simply the proclamation that, through the life and death of Christ and by the power of the Spirit of God, salvation from sin and the knowledge of God are attainable here and now by incorporation into the fellowship of the people of God, a fellowship of living and departed. The future lies in the hands of God, and the more we are enabled to recognise His power active in the world, the less we require to peer into the mysteries of the future. Only a completely unjustifiable scepticism with regard to the past and the present can throw the whole weight of Christian piety upon a restless longing for that which is not and has not been. Christian hope and optimism with regard to the future are grounded upon the lives of the saints, and upon the approved insight into truth preserved and expressed in Christian faith and worship. Hope is thus grounded upon faith in God, Who has wrought mightily and still does work miracles in our midst.

And yet the eschatological language remains an integral element in Christian piety, as the Epistle for Advent Sunday has it admirably: 'And that, knowing the time, that it is high time to awake out of sleep: for now is our salvation nearer than when we believed. The night is far spent, the day is at hand; let us therefore cast off the works of darkness, and let us put on the armour of light.'

I am now shortly concerned with the eschatological language in so far as it is not already fulfilled in the experience of the Ecclesia of God.

The Lady Margaret Professor of Divinity* recently defined the immediate task of Christian theology to be

* Dr Bethune-Baker.

the re-expression of Christian faith in terms of evolution. I would venture to suggest that the task of the Christian theologian is rather to preserve the Christian doctrine of God from the corrupting influence of the dogma of evolution, at least as that doctrine is popularly understood.

There are two essentials necessary for vigorous and healthy religious faith. The first is that God should be regarded as Himself unchanging, and that communion with Him and knowledge of Him be union with and knowledge of One Who is not Himself in a state of flux, and not subject to perpetual transformation. And the second essential is that He should be thought of as active and powerful. To the faithful Christian this active power of God is not exhausted by the thought that the whole evolution of human history or of the physical structure of the universe is the revelation of the power of God. Far more important than this is the belief that God acts catastrophically in human life, that He works miracles, that men are transformed from sin to righteousness, that prayer calls forth an act of God, that it does not merely effect an adaptation to the laws of nature. The God of the Christian religion is a God of miracles. The record of physical miracles with which our Bible is filled is primarily valuable as a description of the God we worship and in Whom we believe, as One Who acts catastrophically and miraculously. The Biblical stories may be, and in many cases undoubtedly are, symbolical stories, but they symbolise a true conception of God, and a genuine experience. To deprive the saint of the conviction that God has acted and does act miraculously in turning the hearts of the unrighteous to the wisdom of the just, and in revealing to them His will, is to deprive Christian piety of its very life blood.

It is at this point that the eschatological language becomes permanently significant and of genuine devotional and intellectual importance. It enshrines and expresses this true and necessary picture of God. For it does but transfer to the macrocosm of the physical universe what has been experienced in the microcosm of the individual and of the Church. God takes up and transforms our helpless, weak, ignorant, sinful lives, and miraculously transforms them into the kingdom of His active love and mercy. Being thus powerful we are bound to think of Him as able so to transform the physical universe, that it may most perfectly serve and express His Will, and be freed from the slavery of the law of death and decay. And, moreover, the more intensely this sense of corruption and decay is felt, the more will a genuine belief in God tend to express itself in eschatological language. Eschatology is, then, one aspect of the Christian picture of God, and when this is recognised we are and ought to be able to use such imagery, and so be protected from the twin myths of gradual progress and evolution, as they are popularly understood.

But it is not only in the fulness of the Christian conception of God that the eschatological imagery may be both valuable and necessary. It is equally important for our moral life. The perception that the present structure of the world and of society is temporary and incomplete, and that it awaits some great catastrophic act of divine transformation, forms the background of thought from which the specifically Christian ideas of goodness have been perceived and realised.

Dissatisfaction has often been expressed that the New Testament contains no explicit teaching concerning war and peace, or the duties of citizenship, or the laws of property, the care of money or the status of slaves, or the upbringing and education of children. Hardly one of the moral problems with which you and I busy ourselves are even mentioned in the New Testament. Some dissatisfied commentators have forced the meaning of our Lord's teaching so as to make it answer the moral questionings of our modern social reformers. But no satisfactory results are gained thereby.

Of course not. These problems are all ethically secondary problems to a Christian. The one fundamental moral problem is what we should still possess if the whole of our world were destroyed to-morrow, and we stood naked before God. The eschatological belief crudely and ruthlessly sweeps away all our little moral busynesses, strips us naked of worldly possessions and worldly entanglements, and asks what survives the catastrophe.

It is only then that the ultimate moral duties stand alone in all their luminous simplicity: Love of God, and Charity to those who, like us, are bereft of that in which they have so confidently trusted.

This is ultimate Ethics, and ultimate Ethics were revealed to us on the background of an eschatological picture of God. It may, moreover, be doubted whether we shall ever perceive moral truth unless we from time to time make such a thought of God our own.

Please do not imagine that this detaches us from the life which we have to live in this world. If it does, we have still much to learn. The point is that only when we have learnt a detachment from earthly possessions can we face the ordinary and secondary moral problems which are presented to us every day, with any hope of judging rightly.

The true function of the Church is to bring men into the presence of God, and to believe confidently that a new love and a new charity will thereby be formed in them. Only when our religion can foster such ultimate morality have we a right to hope that England will be a better country, or that we shall be better citizens, or that employers and employed will work together for the common good, or that parents will adequately provide for the education of their children.

In conclusion I would, therefore, ask you to take very seriously our Christian language and symbolism. It is far more fundamentally true than most people perceive. And the eschatology in particular has implications for Christian belief and morals which are at present almost entirely misunderstood and unrecognised.

II
SIN

(1927–28)

I. SIN AND THE REMISSION
OF SIN

When a Christian man declares that the four-times
repeated response in the Litany of the English Church
—'Have mercy upon us miserable sinners'—has no
meaning for him, he proclaims in public, either that he
has as yet no understanding of the Christian religion,
or that he has apostatised from it.

During this term and next, I propose to attempt the
justification of this very severe judgment by an examination of the language in the New Testament concerning
sin and concerning the remission of sin, and to test
current ideas about God and Christ and the Church in
the light of this language. If the subject appears to you
well-worn or unreal, I would ask you to recall at the
outset certain familiar passages in the New Testament
in which the fact of human sin is grimly exposed.

'If we say that we have no sin, we deceive ourselves,
and the truth is not in us.' (I John i. 8.)

'Behold the Lamb of God, which taketh away the
sin of the world.' (St John i. 29.)

'Jesus came into Galilee, preaching the gospel of
God...repent ye and believe in the gospel.'
(St Mark i. 14, 15.)

'Jesus saith unto the sick of the palsy, Son, thy sins
are forgiven.' (St Mark ii. 5.)

'It is written that repentance and remission of sins
should be preached unto all nations, beginning from
Jerusalem.' (St Luke xxiv. 46, 47.)

'Whosesoever sins ye forgive, they are forgiven unto them; and whosesoever sins ye retain, they are retained.'   (St John xx. 23.)

Unless we have lost all sense of the authority of the New Testament, or are wholly ignorant of it, it is evident that in such passages the very kernel of the Word of God is revealed to us. Moreover, these texts have not been selected with extreme care in order to provide a manipulated impression of the Gospel. Similar sayings occur on almost every page of the New Testament.

If, then, human sin be a well-worn subject, it is well-worn because it belongs to the very structure of our being; and if it appears unreal to us, we are almost certainly the victims of arrogance and self-deceit.

A preacher or a theologian who is ordained to bear witness to the revelation of the power of God needs therefore to offer no excuse for selecting sin, human sin, our sin, as the subject of a connected course of Christian sermons. Did I say 'selecting'? No, he does not select or choose to treat of sin and of the mercy and judgment of God. These are given him, forced upon him by the Bible, by the Church, by the condition of the world in which he lives, and by the passions which stir and move and surge within his own being.

The secularising of the Christian religion lurks like a cancer behind the history of the Church, and from time to time it breaks forth violently, causing great pain and prostration. Then it is that the world invades the Church, attacking it powerfully from without and subtly from within. From one of these virulent attacks we are now suffering, and the disease stalks abroad unashamed, and we are all infected and weakened and crippled. Men of God rush into print wildly and impatiently to deal with this or that point of Christian doctrine or worship; men of science tyrannise dogmatically over us in public and in private; historians, and particularly the historians of comparative religion, increasingly tend to treat the Christian religion as a thing among other things which form the structure of our civilisation, regarding the Church as a section of human society and its teaching as a number of particular, though powerful, ideas; and, finally, psychologists persuade us to consider Christian piety as that which toils up from the obscure recesses within us, but which nevertheless is capable of satisfactory analysis. So we are engulfed in ideas about God, about Christ, about the Bible and the Church, and we listen attentively, sometimes in agreement, sometimes in disagreement, to what Mr Arnold Bennett, what Mr Bertrand Russell, and what other distinguished men think about God or about the Sacraments of the Church. And what the great ones do in public, we imitate in private. We discuss religion, and carry on propaganda, and attempt to do somebody else good—in short, we desire to interfere, and just in so far as we succeed, we cease to proclaim the wonderful works of God.

From one point of view all this activity is healthy and good, it is inevitable. But if this be the whole truth, it ends in our preening and picking our feathers, without doubt or sense of danger, and proudly declaring 'What a fine bird am I!', and this has undoubtedly very little to do with the Christian religion, and may become its direct negation.

Let me be more precise, in order to test the progress of the disease. How do you as Christians think of the poor? Do you conceive of them as in need of something you possess and can give them? Do you imagine that you have advantages of birth, of education, of intelligence, or of money, which can be used for their benefit? Or have you been taught perhaps that they have an experience of life which may be of advantage to you? If all this be true, then we must think of the fellowship of rich and poor in terms of give and take, and no doubt as men of the world we are bound so to think and act. We shall teach, and be generous, and endeavour to do good, and enrich our experience of life in so doing. But as Christians, ought we primarily to think so? Surely not. If this be the ground of Christian fellowship, it is grounded upon arrogance and irreligion. Christian fellowship springs from quite other premises. It springs from the deep-rooted recognition that we all, rich and poor alike, stand under the judgment of God, that we all need His mercy and pity and forgiveness, that—to use Christian language—we are all miserable sinners, and that we have nothing to give them, nor they us. Upon that basis we are all linked together in an indissoluble unity, since we and they are by this recognition inevitably purged of all pride and arrogance.

Or again: How do you think of this Chapel? Is it to you a building among other buildings, a part of the traditional structure of an ancient foundation, a place where certain activities are concentrated, where music is performed, and liturgical experiments are made, where you may, if you will, listen to good or bad or indifferent discourses upon morals or doctrine or faith?

Do you conceive of the services as things in which your predecessors were compelled to share, but at which the governing body of the College does not now demand your attendance, and that therefore you are free men? Of course all this is from one point of view true. Music is made here, we do discourse, and you are completely free to be present or absent. But in the end all this is wide of the mark. This Chapel is the place where the Word of God is proclaimed and the Sacraments are administered, where the power of the living God may touch and enter your life and mine, where we meet together without pride or arrogance in faith that the miracle of freedom from the power and guilt of the evil with which we are contaminated may be wrought in us by God. For freedom, in its Christian sense, is not freedom to do what we like, but freedom from the power and guilt of sin, and such freedom is given, not attained. Are you able to see through all the frailties which are inevitable in any human act of worship, and, perceiving that they are ultimately irrelevant and insignificant, can you recognise that after all this Chapel exists only to proclaim the sovereignty of God, and that the only really impressive action of ours is the complete surrender of ourselves to His regal sovereignty?

'In Jewry is God known; His name is great in Israel.
At Salem is His tabernacle: and His dwelling in Sion.

> There brake he the arrows of the bow:
> the shield, the sword, and the battle.
> Thou art of more honour and might:
> than the hills of the robbers.'

Such vigorous belief in God is the very kernel of the

Christian religion, as it was to the Jewish worshippers in Jerusalem.

We all need a thorough and radical purgation; the purging from the egocentrism, anthropocentrism, which is invading our whole conception of life, and which, if it proceeds far, renders the Christian religion powerless and insignificant: since it is not what we think about God and Christ and the Church and the Scriptures, which in the end matters very much; but rather what God thinks about us, how we are judged by the Christ and by the living Word of God, made manifest in the Scriptures and in the Church.

Would that we clergy might be obedient to the words of St Paul as they are translated in Tyndale's version:

'We preach not ourselves, but Jesus Christe our Lorde. We are not as the most part are who choppe and change with the word of God.'

II. SIN AND THE DEADLY SINS

The busyness with which we all endeavour to expound the verities of the Christian religion without being ourselves humbled under the holiness of God, and without being thereby conscious that both we and those who hear our utterances or read our books are miserable sinners—this busyness is the supreme apostasy from God and the death of true Religion. Apostasy, because Christian perception of truth proceeds, and can only proceed, from the clear recognition that we all stand under the judgment of God: Death, because that life which is peculiarly Christian and which is eternal, proceeds, and can only proceed, from salvation from sin.

(Such was the conclusion reached in the first of this series of addresses concerning Sin and the Remission of Sin.)

Clearly, however, this language will appear nervous and exaggerated unless the word 'sin' can be shewn to possess a meaning more precise and more significant than that which is conveyed in our common and every-day speech.

When a famous modern actress apologises to the readers of her Memoirs for the 'many literary sins' which she knows she must have committed, language ceases to be disciplined, and the word sin is so expanded in meaning as to lose its dignified horror. And when, contrariwise, sin be confined only to denote those furious floods of passion which issue in blind drunkenness or bestial adultery, the word is so limited in meaning as to release the greater number from the necessity of applying it to themselves.

Sin belongs to the language of Religion, and, if it be permitted to stray far from its proper sphere, it is soon confounded with other words and its true meaning is obscured. For example, sin is not a synonym for evil. War is to many an evil because it interrupts the calm progress of trade, or destroys comfort, or involves the sacrifice of life; but it is not for such reasons sin. War is sin only when it can be shewn to be revolt against God.

(And here I cannot resist uttering a protest against the method of keeping Armistice Day into which this

country has drifted. It appears as though we have permitted sorrow for the dead to absorb our observance.
But rejoicing ought to be our chief note of the day,
gratitude for a victory by which our country was freed
from a human threat and a human tyranny. On the
other hand, our horror ought to penetrate far deeper,
till we recognise in war not a thing isolated and peculiar,
but one of the many signs that we all form part of a
world enslaved and in active revolution against the
holiness of God. The mere interruption of a comfortable
security, or supposed security, seems hardly worthy of a
mournful celebration.)

Nor are crime and sin synonymous words. A crime is
properly 'an act punishable by law as being forbidden
by statute or injurious to the public welfare'; the action
is sin only when it is an offence against God. No doubt
the two overlap, but in meaning they are entirely
distinct.

Sin therefore involves God, and the revelation of His
holiness reveals sin. Just in proportion as we are enabled
to perceive the power of the living and righteous God
does our sense of sin grow and develop. If then sin be
revolt against God, it remains for us to endeavour to be
more particular in describing the nature of that revolt.

As Christians we inherit a description in the form of
a catalogue of Deadly Sins, which will repay a more
careful examination than is usually given to formula-
tions received from the Middle Ages, but which in fact
have their roots in the earliest writings of our religion.

The Deadly Sins, that is, sins which destroy us, are
stated to be seven—Pride, Envy, Intemperance, Avarice,

Anger, Lust, and Sloth or Accidie. These were formulated and their number fixed by Peter Lombard, the
Scholastic theologian of the Middle Ages; but Peter was
working upon a tradition reaching back through
Gregory the Great and the *Psychomachia* of Prudentius
to the New Testament itself.

Now the significance of this list may not at first sight
be apparent: partly because we tend, under the influence
of an evil tradition, to regard the Seven Deadly Sins as
actions dependent upon an act of the will, and therefore
to confine Sin to sins which are committed in direct and
conscious defiance of a known and accepted moral law.
This is, however, to misunderstand completely the very
essence of the Christian religion. That we should so
misunderstand it is not surprising, since Western moral
ideas spring largely either from that moral theology
which has been developed under the influence of the
confessional or from that moralism which emerges from
the reflections of philosophers, and in both cases a
wrong action tends to be defined as culpable only when
it is a wilful act. For example, a modern Roman theologian opens his series of volumes on moral theology
with the following definition: 'The terms sin, transgression, iniquity, offence, and disobedience are synony-
mously employed by Holy Scripture to designate a
wilful transgression of the Law of God, or voluntary
disregard of His will.' If we omit the words 'synony-
mously', 'voluntary' and 'wilful', the definition might
stand, but if these be included in the definition, the whole
Christian conception of sin is emasculated at the outset,
and a casual glance at the Seven Deadly Sins shews this
at once. Avarice, which proceeds from the desire of the

possession of material things, and the attachment of the heart to such things, is not a passion which springs from the conscious will: it is part of our very being as men of flesh and blood, it surges up within us. So is Anger, so is Lust, so are Pride and Envy. We do not create these things by our wills. They rise and submerge us. The conscious wilful voluntary action is the least serious element, since it does but make manifest the underlying forces which course within us.

We must rid our minds of this paralysing idea that sins are a series of forbidden actions which we can, if we will, avoid. Sin is this world, with its desires and passions, running its course till ultimately we lie dead, a corpse, the material world having won its victory and itself then passing to corruption. Death is therefore the complete and adequate symbol of sin, and Accidie or Sloth is the runner-up of death.

But we must not think of sin merely in terms of the material world. The catalogue itself forbids this. Pride, *Superbia*, majestically heads the list, followed by Envy. Here we are on another plane, far more subtle, and far more devastating. Pride is the capital sin, the sin which controls our minds and heads, not our bodies merely. Pride belongs to us when we become the centre of the Universe, when everything revolves about us and everything is judged as it affects us, when our achievements dominate our ideas. And Envy is Pride's younger sister, that sadness which occupies us when others intrude into that central position which we imagine to be ours. And Pride is atheism, just as Lust is barbarism; for Pride is not merely jealousy of other men, it is inevitably jealousy of God. It is intolerable to us that God should

stand at the centre of the Universe and not man, that
we should be His creation, and depend upon Him, or
that He should control our destiny.

So we protect ourselves against God and fight against
that utter humiliation before Him which He demands.
And, since the Christian religion is simply this submission, we hate the Church and the Scriptures, and we
dislike the clergy who perpetually, though often unconsciously, remind us of our insignificance. Or, more
acutely and diabolically, we persuade ourselves that
religion, the Christian religion, is humanitarianism.
For Pride is not merely individual: Pride rears its head
when human achievement, human knowledge, human
love and affection are identified with the Christian
religion, and when 'God' becomes another word for
'man'. This is naked atheism, and it is atheism pro-
ceeding from Pride—the ultimate blasphemy. Can you
now see why Pride is far more serious than adultery?
Adultery and such gross vices are, thanks be to God, still
obviously to the majority evil things; they carry their
own condemnation. But Pride is so inevitably so much
a part of our common humanity, that it escapes us, and
we fail to recognise it. It invades the Church, interprets
the Scriptures, and dethrones God.

It is the sin from which all other sin proceeds, and it
can be detected in its full enormity only by those to
whom God has revealed Himself, and who therefore
stand under His judgment.

'The heavens declare the glory of God and the
firmament sheweth his handiwork.'

'And the Word became flesh and dwelt among us, and we beheld his glory, the glory of the only begotten Son of God, full of grace and truth.'

III. SIN IN THE GOSPELS

Sin, then, is human society in revolt against God, and we are controlled by it both as men and as individuals. Sin is majestic, penetrating, deadly. Majestic, because it manifests itself supremely not in Lust, but in Pride; penetrating, because it cannot be limited to actions which proceed from our voluntary choice; deadly, because, if our lives revolve around ourselves alone, they revolve around that which is mortal and passing to inevitable destruction. Death is the revelation of the nature of sin.

'O death, where is thy sting?
O grave, where is thy victory?
The sting of death is sin.'
(I Corinthians xv. 55, 56.)

'And I looked, and behold a pale horse: and his name that sat on him was Death, and Hell followed with him.' (Revelation vi. 8.)

Such were the conclusions drawn from examination of the catalogue of Deadly Sins, which the Church presents to its sons in order to make clear to them the wiles and the power of the Enemy who is set against them, and who makes his palace within them.

It is now necessary to ask whether the Christian delineation of this all-embracing revolt against God belongs to the Gospels, or whether it is but another instance of the supposed contradiction between the teaching of the Church and the teaching of our Lord.

The question is capable of quite precise statement. Does the Gospel proclaimed by our Lord rest upon the perception that life as it is, human life, is apostasy from God, and that therefore men stand under His Κρίσις or Judgment, or does the teaching of Jesus presume a more generous, humanitarian, friendly background?

The latter has been judged to be the true picture of our Lord's teaching by many modern interpreters of the New Testament, and their portrait of Jesus of Nazareth has been widely accepted as freeing the modern world from the tyranny of St Paul, and from the grimmer aspects both of Catholicism and of the Older Evangelicalism, and therefore as relieving us from the necessity of taking seriously the denunciations which fill so many pages of the Old Testament.

> 'Babylon is fallen, is fallen,
> and all the graven images of her gods
> He hath broken to the ground.
> That which I have heard of the Lord of Hosts,
> The God of Israel,
> Have I declared unto you.'
>
> (Isaiah xxi. 9, 10.)

Self-complacently we are told that these words, and words of similar meaning, are not the words of God, but the anger of a Hebrew prophet fulminating against a Babylon which crumbled to pieces centuries ago, and that the gods of Babylon were Bel and Nebo and such like forgotten deities whom you and I are not tempted to worship; and that therefore the passage from the Book of Isaiah does not concern us; it is part of an historical document, which may be of interest to Orientalists and pedantic theologians, and perhaps to fastidious literary gentlemen who presume to admire the vigour of the prophet's language without the necessity of being seriously disturbed by its meaning.

And then the justification for this neglect for the sincere Christian is the contrasted picture of the teaching of Jesus. He, we are informed, unlike the prophets of Israel, unlike even John the Baptist, accepted the world, loved the simple homely life of the Galilean peasants, drew His parables from the carpenter's shop and from the life of the farmer, sat among the lilies, saw the beauty of the sunset, and wandered over the mountain side. To Him life was the manifestation of the love of God. He dined with the rich, conversed with the poor, be-friended the tax-gatherers and the harlots. He abused, it is true, the Pharisees, but only because they did not love their fellow men, or perceive that the poor and outcast were the sons of their Father which is in heaven. So Jesus looked round upon the world of nature and of men, and proclaimed that God is love.

Fascinating the portrait is, but is it true? Was this the Jesus of the Gospel story? If He were so, then we must be honest. Humanitarianism is the Gospel: let us arise as Christians and tear up the Old Testament, consign the Epistles of St Paul to the flames, forget St Augustine, and transform the Church, or destroy it if it be not possible to change it.

But before we embark on so hazardous an enterprise, we should be quite certain of the ground of our revolt.

Is the interpretation we have put upon our Gospels a justifiable interpretation? Is the background of our Lord's words and actions a generous acceptance of the multifarious activities of human life, so that the world of nature and of men is the expression of the beneficent power of active divine love?

A decisive answer to this question is impossible apart from some familiarity with the literary criticism of the Gospels. We do not possess in the four Gospels four independent narratives of our Lord's life. St Mark's Gospel is an original literary creation which was used by the other three Evangelists, and even the author of the Fourth Gospel knew and made use of St Mark. The importance of St Mark's Gospel was probably due to the knowledge that it represented the teaching of St Peter. In addition to St Mark's Gospel St Luke and St Matthew knew and made use of another document which has not survived. This Lost Document, which is called Q, seems to have consisted of a more or less orderly arrangement of sayings of Jesus, and all our evidence goes to shew that it was completely independent of St Mark's Gospel. And it is not unreasonable to suppose that it was written by an Apostle, perhaps by St Matthew, since our Matthew is clearly the work of an editor, and the name may be the result of a transference of name from a literary source to the later compilation, in which St Matthew's work had been used.

The result of this literary analysis is that the historian is on comparatively sure ground when Mark and the passages which are common to Matthew and Luke but which are not in Mark—i.e. passages from Q—overlap and describe the same teaching, or when they agree in assuming a common background to our Lord's words.

Now this means that certain parts of our Gospel tradition, which the ordinary reader barely notices, become of prime importance because they stood originally both in Mark and in Q, in the two original independent apostolic documents.

The result of the most critical analysis of the Synoptic Gospels leaves certain passages as undoubtedly historical. The relevant passage which is thrust upon our attention as a result of this literary analysis is the great Beelzebul speech. Its prime importance lies in the discovery that it belongs to the earliest strata of the Gospel tradition, and that in it is preserved our Lord's interpretation of His mission.

In St Mark's Gospel, the Beelzebul speech follows immediately the call of the twelve Apostles, and interprets the significance of their selection; in Matthew, it interprets the significance of the healing of a man who was both blind and dumb; in Luke, it interprets the healing of a dumb man. Presumably, therefore, in Q it was introduced in order to explain the general importance of our Lord's miracles of healing.

Our Lord healed men and women, and called His disciples to Him. Well, what does this energetic action mean? That is what we are meant to ask, and the Beelzebul speech is our Lord's answer to that question. His human relatives say He is mad, and endeavour to draw Him back from the crowds to the privacy and security of domestic life. The Scribes and Pharisees make the judgment of our Lord's family more precise.

Yes, He is mad, and madness means that He is empowered by Beelzebul the prince of the demons. It is a grim and terrible moment, and our Lord is forced to deal firmly with this drastic and subtle attempt to interfere with His work. But we are hardly prepared for what follows. His language is parabolic, but its meaning is evident. The Devil is the Lord of the House, that is the literal meaning of the name Beelzebul; men and women are his goods, his property; they serve his ends. There is only one possibility of their release from this slavery. The Devil must be bound, as a successful thief must bind the owner if he is to steal his property. The stronger than the Devil must come and bind him with shackles; only so can men and women be rescued from his power. The Lord then proclaims that He is the thief of the Devil's property, the stronger than the Power of evil. And His miracles, of healing, blind men seeing, and deaf men hearing, disciples obeying the call to follow Him, are manifestations, signs that the Messiah has come, that the Devil is dethroned, and his goods purloined. The words of Isaiah are literally fulfilled.

'Shall the prey be taken from the mighty one
or the (lawful) captive be delivered?
Thus saith the Lord.
Aye, the captives of the mighty shall be taken away
and the prey of the terrible shall be delivered:
for I will contend with him that contendeth with thee,
and I will save thy children.'   (Isaiah xlix. 24 ff.)

Where is the madness then? The crowds, the madness lies there: not in Jesus. Men and women are distraught under the tyranny of sin, which is slavery to the Evil

One, and the Lord is the Messiah, the hope of their salvation.

Now I ask you to think what this means. Where is the Jesus, who has been presented for our humanitarian and democratic admiration? Where is the figure of One to Whom human life is the reflection of the love of God; Who sees the homely beauty of Galilean peasant life, and rests in that beauty? It is not there in our Gospel tradition. And the modern picture of the friendly attitude to human life is just humbug; it is, I dare to say it, fudge. And if we read the Gospels with dark spectacles firmly fixed upon our noses, we shall never perceive the meaning of the Christian religion; we shall remain blind and deaf, and it would be better if we were also dumb.

IV. SIN AND THE CRUCIFIXION

When John Sebastian Bach sought to give musical expression to the very kernel of Christian truth, he turned to the Mass for his words. The B minor Mass opens with the poignant cry of the whole chorus and orchestra, Kyrie Eleison, Lord have mercy, and in the fugue which follows all the voices and instruments independently take up the theme; there are no other words, simply Kyrie Eleison.

No one who has ever heard it can doubt that in that universal cry for mercy we are led to the threshold of our religion. Nor is it merely a preliminary; the sense of utter human unworthiness is the permanent ground bass through which the melody of the gospel of the mercy of God sounds in our ears, so that the suitable epitaph for a Christian is composed of two words only, 'Jesu, mercy'. This is far more impressive, far more Christian, than a catalogue of virtues, or of benevolent actions, or of intellectual achievements.

This overwhelming recognition of human sin controls the Old Testament and the New Testament alike, and no understanding of our Lord's words and actions is possible if we persist in denying it.

Further, the Gospels are filled with narratives of miraculous healings. Our fathers found great difficulty in such miracles, and a controversy arose as to whether the miraculous elements in the Gospels were historical or not. The controversy is not relevant, at least so far as the majority of the miracles of healing are concerned, since they present no real difficulty. That our Lord healed all kinds of physical diseases causes the modern commentator no uneasy moments. It is therefore widely supposed that the miracles of healing must be added to the historical substratum of the story of the life of Jesus, and that is that. We are then left to suppose that our Lord was touched by the sight of suffering and that by the power of His faith He was enabled to alleviate the pain of certain cripples, and that a few more incidents of kind actions must therefore be added to the history of humanitarianism, and that the Church, if it be the Church of Christ, must be persuaded to undertake more seriously the support of doctors in their work of healing disease.

Now, there is no doubt much truth in this, but it rests on an almost completely false interpretation of the significance of our Lord's miracles of healing as they are narrated in the Gospels. The question we are meant to ask is not, Did they happen? (that is comparatively irrelevant), but, What did they mean to our Lord? and what, therefore, do they mean to us?

At the opening of St Mark's Gospel the author records the healing of a paralytic. You know the story. His friends let him down through the roof, and there he lies motionless, the complete symbol of life rendered useless. He is publicly released from the power of the disease and walks through the crowd carrying his bed. If you really think that is the story, you can surely have never read it. In fact, our Lord solemnly pronounces the man to be a sinner, and the whole narrative is woven round the words 'Son, thy sins have been forgiven thee', 'The Son of man hath authority on earth to remit sins' or, perhaps better, to 'release from sins'. There is not the least suggestion in the narrative that the man was especially wicked. The whole incident is recorded as of vital concern, not merely for the man who was healed, but for the whole crowd of onlookers including the Scribes who sat with their hearts full of 'evil imaginings'. The incident simply reveals to all, both who saw and who read the narrative, the mercy of God Who alone is able to release men from the power of the Evil One.

There are none who have achieved so lofty a pinnacle of righteousness, that they can afford to contemplate the miracle as one which does not concern them.

To the story of the healing of the paralytic, St Mark adds as a pendant the account of the call of Levi, the publican, and his answer to the call. Here we have a case of a man rescued from a disease where there are no physical complications. He is simply detached by our Lord from the world, and the significance of the whole section of the narrative is summed up in the words, 'I came not to call the righteous but sinners'—Luke adds, 'to repentance'. It is surely clear from the whole teaching of our Lord that no one of those who composed the crowds but needed repentance, or was excused from the necessity of following Him. Nor is it otherwise when we consider the sayings of our Lord preserved in the Lost Document (Q) which, as we have seen, underlies our Gospel tradition, and the contents of which are known to us from Luke and Matthew who both extracted much of their material from it.

In Q, the miracles of Jesus are not kind actions done to isolated poor men: they are manifestations of a New Order bursting forth among men, signs that the Kingdom of God has come and that the Messiah has appeared. The miracles betray the advent of the mercy of God. When John sent from prison to know whether Jesus were the Christ, our Lord's answer was, 'Go tell John what ye see and hear; the blind see, the lame walk, the deaf hear, the dead are raised and to the poor the good news is being preached'.

But in spite of the miracles the story moves relentlessly on. The Christ is rejected, and Q contains the dreadful saying, 'To what shall I liken the world of men and women? They are like children sitting in the market place, which cry to their companions, we piped to you and you did not dance, we wept and you did not mourn.' The crowd goes on its way unaffected, completely careless. The Baptist came and they put him in prison, the Messiah came and they say, a gluttonous man and a wine-bibber, the friend of publicans and sinners.

So there runs through the story of the life of the Lord the contrast between the world of nature revealing the miraculous acts of God, the birds and the flowers and the trees obedient to their Creator, but men busy, active, immersed, proud, independent, blind to the call of the God Who made them and Who with infinite long-suffering continues to give them the rain and the sun, imagining that they are the centre of the universe, measuring, judging, weighing everything in balances. But all the while it is they who are being weighed in the balances—and found wanting.

Can you bear more from this dreadful book the New Testament? There is worse to come. 'And they crucified Him.' There is no one innocent, no not one. The disciples all forsook Him and fled. The two criminals crucified with Him railed on Him and died: that is our earliest tradition. The crowd led by these otherwise learned and reputable people the Pharisees, the best of the Jews, surrounded the Cross and laughed at the Christ, and Pilate, rather disgusted, is quite helpless. Whatever else the Crucifixion is, it is a most humiliating scene, humiliating not, please, so much for our Lord, as for us men; that is the kind of thing we, you and I, do left to ourselves. The Cross is to us Christians fundamentally the symbol of human inadequacy, it is the revelation of the horror of sin, more horrible because none of those who crucified Him knew what they were doing.

Now what is the conclusion from all this? First, Redemption and Salvation are Christian words. The Gospel is contained in them. As men we are in need of release and remission of sins. Secondly, there is no reason to suppose that our redemption can be evolved from ourselves.

> 'O put not your trust in princes,
> nor in any child of man,
> for there is no help in them.
> For when the breath of man goeth forth,
> he shall turn again to his earth;
> and then all his thoughts perish.'
>
>   (Psalms cxlvi. 3, 4.)

It is a hard truth for us to learn, we in the pride of our achievements, we with our doctrines of evolution, we with our petty impertinence convinced that God can only speak to men through men, through human personalities. If we are to become Christians we must learn to see through all this modern make-believe, and return to the old Christian language of the Advent of God. The Church, the Bible, the bread and wine of the Eucharist, in fact the Christ, there, if we have eyes to see it, is the active creative Word of God, there is the point at which the other world, the power of the omnipotent God touches this world. The kingdom of God upon earth, the eschatology, the end of history, remission of sin.

V. SIN AND THE FORGIVENESS OF SIN

Thus we all stand under the judgment of God, with nothing in our hands, neither righteousness in virtue of which we can stand upright in His presence, nor knowledge possessing which we are enabled to pry into His innermost secrets and to criticise His government of the world. And Sin is the word by which we denote our failure to perceive the vast chasm which separates the Creator from the creature, which separates God and man. 'For my thoughts are not your thoughts, neither are my ways your ways, saith the Lord.' Sin is discovered in all its crudity when we are engulfed by the material world with its desires and passions and lusts, or, far more subtly, when we exalt our petty morality and our limited intelligence so that upon these twin pillars we build up our Tower of Babel, and, mounted upon its topmost storey, we proudly survey or dethrone God, as though He were an object for our self-satisfied contemplation or a truth for us to discover. This is the old Pelagian heresy, that heresy which is hardly worthy to be called a heresy, because a heresy is an exaggeration of some one Christian verity, and Pelagianism—the belief that we can, as men, achieve a righteousness which is pleasing to God, or that we can evolve the knowledge of God—is simply a belief vacant of any Christian content whatsoever: it is in fact a penetrating and completely adequate definition of sin. Now Pelagianism in its modern dress threatens to invade and conquer our whole conception of religion, by fixing our attention upon the busyness of men and women, rather than by insisting upon the necessity of the surrender of ourselves to the goodness and the mercy and indeed to the severity of God. Only when this Pelagian Tower of Babel, in which we are so confidently placing our trust, is cast to the ground can God reveal Himself to us as individual men, or to that society in which we live.

Sin, then, is our presumption in the presence of God or of that which He has set before us as a means or vehicle for the revelation of His power and goodness. Sin is, therefore, the preference of that which we control to that which is controlled by God; it is the preference of self-government to the rule of God. Sin is Pride, and Pride belongs to our innermost being, and it is for us Christians manifested, declared and revealed in all its nakedness in the Crucifixion of our Lord.

This was the conclusion which we reached at the end of last term.

And yet I would not have you conclude that the Christian and Jewish recognition of human sin is to be confused with that disillusionment or scepticism about human life which disfigures so many modern novels, and which turns men into cynics, or pictures them as the playthings of Fate. Of that virtue, which is the reward of painstaking self-discipline or the result of a noble heritage, and of that knowledge which proceeds from long concentration of energy or from a lively intuition, our religion is neither cynical nor critical. It is critical only when such virtue or such knowledge leads to tyranny over others or to presumption towards God. Such selfishness is not merely criticised, it is roundly declared to be sin, blasphemous sin, the root of all evil.

From this blasphemous and tyrannical sin we pray that
we may be delivered.

Now where in all this is the Gospel? The Gospel is
revealed already with piercing directness in the Old
Testament. Crisply in the opening verses of the great
chapters at the end of the book of the Prophet Isaiah:

'Ho, everyone that thirsteth, come ye to the waters,
   and he that hath no money; come ye, buy, and eat;
   Yea, come, buy wine and milk
   without money and without price.' (Isaiah lv. 1.)

'Sing, O barren, thou that didst not bear;
   Break forth into singing, and cry aloud,
   thou that didst not travail with child:
   For more are the children of the desolate
   than the children of the married wife, saith the Lord.'
                            (Isaiah liv. 1.)

There in vigorous imagery the good news is proclaimed. Just at the point where men and women
possess nothing, no money, no children, there, where all
pride of possession is annihilated, there breaks forth the
mercy of God.

'Arise, shine: for thy light is come,
   and the glory of the Lord is risen upon thee.'

Poignantly the same truth is uttered in the twenty-
second Psalm:

'My God, my God, look upon me; why hast thou forsaken me:
 and art so far from my health, and from the words of
   my complaint?

O my God, I cry in the day time, but thou hearest not:
and in the night season also I take no rest.
As for me, I am a worm, and no man:
a very scorn of men, and the outcast of the people.
My strength is dried up like a potsherd, and my tongue
    cleaveth to my gums.'

There is the complete humiliation before God. But
listen to what follows:

'Thou hast heard me also from among the horns of the
    unicorns.
O praise the Lord . . .
For the kingdom is the Lord's: and he is the governour
    among the people.'

It is, however, in the Book of Job that the truth is
most clearly revealed; for it is there that the undertones
of the Old Testament become a clearly defined melody.
And yet we are persistently taught to misunderstand
the book. The phrase 'the patience of Job' has done
much to darken our understanding, since, of course, his
impatience forms the main theme until the final conclusion of the book. Nor are we placed in a better
position when we are told that the Book of Job is a
disquisition on the problem of the suffering of the
righteous, as though Job were an innocent man who is
bullied by three very superficial friends. The truth is
that Job is not merely impatient, he is the supreme
concretion of ultimate blasphemy, who will not listen
to advice, until God Himself takes the matter into His
own hands.

Job has lost his children, his property, and his health.

One thing alone he guards jealously—his pride. There he sits on a heap of ashes scraping himself with a potsherd, and for thirty-five chapters blasphemy after blasphemy and cursing upon cursing proceed from his mouth. It is all directed against God. Nothing matters in the world but his sense of injustice, every word he speaks is completely self-centred. His fate is a blot upon the character of God. The day of his birth ought to be erased from the calendar.

> 'Let the day perish wherein I was born....
> Let a cloud dwell upon it....
> Let it not come into the number of the months.
> Lo, let that night be barren.'   (Job iii. 3–7.)

He then ruthlessly sets aside his friends.

> 'No doubt but ye are the people,
> and wisdom shall die with you.
> But I have understanding as well as you;
> I am not inferior to you....
> Ye are forgers of lies.'   (Job xii. 2, 3; xiii. 4.)

It is not with them he would argue, but with God. He is completely innocent, and he wishes to tell that to God face to face and challenge Him even though he may be killed for his heroism. "I am perfect, and if He kill me for saying so, well, I despise my life, but I will tell Him the truth and die for it." But God will not appear and be insulted. He then wishes there were some umpire between him and God. He is right, God is wrong, and any impartial observer would say so. 'There is no daysman' (the old English word for umpire or arbiter) 'between us that he might lay his hand upon us both'.

There is no impartial observer, and God refuses to play
the game and appear and be convinced that Job is right
and God is wrong.

> 'Surely I would speak to the Almighty
> And I desire to reason with God.'

And so it goes on and on. He has a right against God,
and He must protect him against these pettifogging
pseudo-theologians. But they are mainly in the right,
and Job is wrong, heroically wrong, it is true. *Finally
God reveals Himself*, and Job's pride is completely crushed.
He ceases to protest his innocence, and his desire for an
argument with God evaporates into nothingness. The
Tower of Babel is swept to the ground.

> Then God answered Job out of the whirlwind:
> 'Who is this that darkeneth counsel
> by words without knowledge?
> Gird up thy loins like a man;
> For I will demand of thee, and declare thou unto me.
> Where wast thou when I laid the foundation of the
>   earth?...
> Doth the hawk soar by thy wisdom?
> Doth the eagle mount up at thy command?...
> Shall he that cavilleth contend with the Almighty?
> He that argueth with God, let him answer it.'
>   (Job xxxviii. 2–4; xxxix. 26, 27; xl. 2.)

> Then Job answered:
> 'Behold I am of small account.
> Once I have spoken...
> yea twice, but I will proceed no further.'
>   (Job xl. 4, 5.)

Then the Lord answered Job again out of the whirl-wind:

'Gird up thy loins now like a man...
Declare thou unto me.
Wilt thou even disannul my judgment?
Wilt thou condemn me, that thou mayest be justified?
Hast thou an arm like God?'   (Job xl. 7–9.)

'Canst thou subdue the hippopotamus (Behemoth)
or the crocodile (Leviathan)?
If thou canst then will I confess
that thine own right hand can save thee.'

(Job xl. 14.)

And Job answered and said:

'I had heard of thee by the hearing of the ear:
But now mine eye seeth thee.
Wherefore I abhor myself, and repent in dust and
    ashes.'   (Job xlii. 5, 6.)

When once Job has said this, at that point, the love and the mercy of God is poured out upon him. And the book ends at once with the rather crude picture of Job's prosperity restored and increased.

Understand the Book of Job, and we are on the threshold of the New Testament, on the threshold of the Christian religion. For—let me put it roughly—at the moment of the Crucifixion there bursts upon the world —will you be shocked?—there emerges—the Church, the Ecclesia of God.

But this apparent paradox needs much explanation.

VI. SIN AND THE CHURCH

Can we rescue a word, and discover a universe? Can we study a language, and awake to the Truth? Can we bury ourselves in a lexicon, and arise in the presence of God? A word is of delicate structure, and often we bend it and wound it, until it is so disfigured that it only survives by growing coarse and haggard and debauched. And in this sad history we are impoverished; for with the loss of a word, a thing, a memory or a truth passes beyond us, and we are wounded and crippled and coarsened by our inability to recover it. Thus it may happen that the historian regains his balance only as he turns to decipher the meanings of words, and the theologian escapes from the sand only as he follows a phrase to its source. Before advancing further I must therefore bother you with a philological digression; and repeat what is to many familiar and well worn.

That the word *Church* in the English language has seriously surrendered its nobility, is made apparent from the ugly words we have built upon it. A few citations will make this abundantly clear. 'The very air of the place is redolent with churchiness.' 'The new High Churchites who want to turn all quiet people adrift.' 'His politics are benevolent, conservative and, above all, Churchy.' 'Some of the queer narrowness of English Churchism.' 'Men who were shut out from the English Universities by their Tests and Churchified influence.' Such word-building hardly veils the assumption that devotion to the Church is to be sharply distinguished from devotion to Christ, so that even the word 'Church-man' is to our ears less dignified than the word 'Christian'. But what is the meaning of the word 'Church' or 'Kirk' or 'Kirche' or the Russian 'Cerkov'? It is simply the Slavonic and the Teutonic adaptation of the Greek word κυριακόν, meaning *belonging to the Lord*, and it denotes that which peculiarly reveals God or Christ in the world, or which reminds us of His power and truth and mercy and goodness.

As with the word *Church*, so it is with the even more significant word 'Ecclesia' from which we have manu-factured the modern meaning of the words Ecclesiastic and Ecclesiastical: listen to their use. 'He had in him much of the taste and temper of the ecclesiastic.' 'A final grapple with ecclesiastical tyranny.' 'His was a character extremely familiar in the annals of ecclesiasti-cism.' I doubt whether in ordinary conversation we could use these words without a somewhat sinister suggestion. But what a perversion it all is, and what a history lurks behind the word ἐκκλησία! Preserved in the West, it is at first sight just a Greek survival. But, if so, why did it survive, and why was it incapable of translation? Ἐκκλησία in Greek means merely a regularly convoked assembly, and if that were all that the word suggested, it was capable of entirely adequate translation into Latin by *convocatio* or *congregatio*, and when we required a word in English to translate ἐκκλησία there was no need for our fathers to have adopted the irrelevant word Church, when Congregation would have entirely sufficed. But the word ἐκκλησία survived in the West, in all the Roman and in all the Celtic languages, in the French *église* and in the Gaelic *eglais*, and there is nothing careless in this history of a con-sistent refusal to translate. The early Latin Fathers tried to translate the word, but found it impossible. St Augustine nearly succeeded with his *Civitas Dei*, the City of God, but the phrase merely suggests to us his own great volume.

The truth is that around the word *ecclesia* there had gathered a wealth of suggestion and allusion which attached to none of its secular equivalents, and therefore it survived, at first the effective, and later the ineffective symbol of its peculiar history.

In form the word is Greek, in content it is Hebraic, Old Testament, Jewish. In the Septuagint or Greek translation of the Old Testament Scriptures, the word *ecclesia* scarcely veils the Hebrew word *Qāhāl* and reproduces its emphatic consonants: Qahal—ἐκκλησία. But whereas the Greek word means 'called forth for a political purpose', the Hebrew word Qahal denotes the people of God, Israel, chosen by God, selected from all the peoples of the earth to be His own, brought into an especial relationship with Him. Without the wealth of Assyria or of the riches of Egypt, without the skill of Babylon or the learning of Greece, ruling no empire such as fell to the lot of the Hittites or the Romans, humiliated, crushed, hauled into captivity in the rich valley of the Nile or in the even richer valley of the Euphrates, disobedient, sinful, they wandered in the desert, they went a-whoring after other gods, they were corrupted by the Canaanites, Hellenised by the half-heathen House of Herod—and yet the people of God, His Qahal or ἐκκλησία, possessing His oracles, yoked to His law, providing His prophets and preachers and sometimes submitting to the government of kings who ruled in His name, aye, even in their uttermost weakness

revealing the Majesty of the Lord of Hosts, the Creator
of the world and of men.

And the prophet Isaiah sees the meaning of all this
paradoxical history, and trembles on the brink of something which goes beyond it when he records the judgment of the secular despots upon the people of Israel.

'He hath no form nor comeliness;
  and when we see him, there is no beauty
        that we should desire him.
He was despised, and rejected,
A man of sorrows, and acquainted with grief...
As one from whom men hide their face
  He was despised,
  And we esteemed him not.
He was oppressed... as a lamb is led to the slaughter...
By oppression... he was taken away.
They made his grave with the wicked.'
                              (Isaiah liii. 2–9.)

This was Israel, the Qahal or ἐκκλησία of God;
this was the Church which belonged to the Lord, and
when they were gathered together they formed the
assembly or ἐκκλησία of Jehovah.

'And the chiefs of all the people, even of all the
tribes of Israel, presented themselves in the Qahal of
the people of God, four hundred thousand footmen
that drew sword.'   (Judges xx. 2.)

'And the spirit of the Lord came upon Jahaziel...
the Levite, in the midst of the Qahal.'
                              (II Chronicles xx. 14.)

'My God, my God...I will declare thy Name unto my
　　brethren.
In the midst of the Qahal will I praise thee.
Ye that fear the Lord, praise him.
All ye the seed of Jacob, glorify him.'
(Psalm xxii. 22, 23.)

'And the High Priest went down and lifted up his
　　hands
over the whole Qahal of the children of Israel,
to give blessing unto the Lord with his lips
and to glory in his name.'　　　(Ecclesiasticus l. 20.)

'In the Qahal of the Most High God
shall wisdom open her mouth
and shall glory in the midst of her people.'
(Ecclesiasticus xxiv. 2.)

In the history of the people of Israel, therefore, the
word Qahal, which originally was but a humble Semitic
word for a congregation or assembly of people, became
ennobled to express what is unique and peculiar, the
throng of the people of God, His home or house upon
earth: and the Greek word ἐκκλησία when brought in
to translate it shares in its special nobility; in the words
Ecclesiasticus or *Ecclesiastes* it survives as the title of two
Old Testament books, and means the man who bears
witness to the Wisdom of God; and this is the entirely
correct and proper meaning of the word Ecclesiastic,
Koheleth, one who belongs to the Qahal of God, and
declares its truth.

And so the word ἐκκλησία lost its indefinite article,
not *an* ecclesia, but *the* Ecclesia—the Ecclesia of God.

And now the second and greater ennobling or consecration of the word ἐκκλησία.

From the Crucifixion of the Lord there emerged in the world the new ἐκκλησία of God, but yet so intimately linked to the old, that the Old Testament remained the authoritative book, the word of God, and the vast vocabulary of the people of Israel survived, invested with a new power and dignity, and the new people of God, not many wise after the flesh, not many mighty, not many noble were summoned, called, elected (κλητοί) into the ἐκκλησία of God; but God chose the foolish things of the world, that he might put to shame them that are wise, and God chose the weak things of the world that he might put to shame the things that are strong; and the base things of the world and the things that are despised did God choose, yea, and the things that are not, that he might bring to nought the things that are, that no flesh should boast itself before God (I Corinthians i. 26 ff.).

And into this Ecclesia or Church which is the gift of God to the world through the death of Christ we have been born by baptism, the people of God, Ecclesiastics, men of the Ecclesia, possessing the oracles of God and remission of sin, separated from the world and called to be saints, clerics—κλῆροί—or God's property.

> 'Hear ye this, O house of Jacob,
>   which are called by the name of Israel,
>   and are come forth out of the waters of Judah;
>   which swear by the Name of the Lord,
>   and make mention of the God of Israel,
>   *But not in truth nor in righteousness.*'

There is the terrible 'But'—'but not in truth nor in righteousness.'

And so we are brought back again from the Ecclesia and in the Ecclesia itself to Sin and to the Remission of Sin.

VII. SIN AND THE REMISSION OF SIN

And so we have reached one of those paradoxes which meet us when we start to grapple with the meaning of our Faith. The Church is set in the midst of the world, in direct opposition to it. And we rightly use language which emphasises the contrast, till perhaps we are led to quote St Paul to make our meaning clear. Outside the Ecclesia of God men are dead through their trespasses and sins, wherein they walk according to the course of this world, according to the prince of the power of the air, sons of unbelief and disobedience, swayed by the lusts of the flesh and inflamed by evil imaginings, without hope and without God in the world. And on the other hand, through the love of God with which He loved us, and quickened us and raised us, and set us in the heavenly places, we are His workmanship, created for good works, fellow citizens with the saints, of the household of God, built upon the foundation of the apostles and prophets, stones fitted together to make the temple of the Lord in the midst of the world.

And yet the moment we have said this we must take it all back. In the Ecclesia of God we struggle and fight, not with the world but with our brothers and sisters in the Church. 'It hath been signified to me that there are contentions among you. Now this I mean that each one of you saith, I am of Paul; and I of Apollos; and I of Cephas; and I of Christ. Are ye not men?' Yes, we are men, and not angels. Men of flesh and blood, not merely quarrelling, but swayed by unworthy passions and desires. And St Paul can write even after his conversion, 'Not what I would that do I practise, but what I hate, that I do. For I delight in the law of God after the inward man: but I see a different law in my members, warring against the law of my mind, and bringing me into captivity under the law of sin which is in my members. O wretched man that I am!'

That is the tragic paradox. The Church separated from the world and yet not only in it, but of it.

Can you see that the word Church is a more real word than the word Christian? A Christian means a man who exhibits the spirit, and follows the precepts and example of Christ. 'To be a Christian', wrote Dean Farrar, 'is to act as Christ acted.' Can you or I dare to arrogate to ourselves such a title? or can we even accept its application to ourselves without indignant repudiation? How rarely the word Christian occurs in the New Testament compared with the word Church! And this is significant. The word Church as we have seen suggests the people of Israel, sinful, disobedient, thoroughly unsatisfactory, and yet possessing the revealed Law of God, chosen by God to proclaim not their goodness or their righteousness but His power and His mercy. So it is

with the Church. We do not claim anything for ourselves. We, as those outside, are under the judgment of
God. But as men of His Ecclesia, we possess the word of
God; we proclaim Christ Crucified, the power of God
and the wisdom of God; we share in the worship of God
in spirit and in truth. We are, or we should be, witnesses
to the truth, with no real confidence in our power to
explain or interpret according to the wisdom of men,
with no desire to set up ourselves as models of righteousness, but confident that the revelation of God, I will not
say *stands* in the Bible, in the sacraments, in the creeds
and in the Christ, but occurs, acts, is energetic and
effective through them.

This is what St Paul and what our Lord meant by the
word Mystery. A mystery is that which reveals the
secret and invisible power of the Unseen God. The
structure of the world is a mystery. That does not mean
it is beyond our comprehension, though of course it is:
it means that it is a revelation of the power of God. The
invisible things of God, His everlasting power and
divinity, says St Paul, are perceived through the structure of the universe. The parables of the Lord are in this
correct sense mysteries, they reveal the Kingdom of God.
So too the Church is the revelation of God. But you and
I are unfortunately not mysteries, at least I do not know
of such an application of the word. We are the objects
of the mercy of God, points to which His power is
directed: not vehicles of revelation, for we obstruct it
and obscure it. And so I would urge you not to assess
the power of God by measuring and weighing the
righteousness of those who believe, and setting it in the
scales against the righteousness of those who stand out-

side the Ecclesia of God. Judge not that ye be not judged, and condemn not that ye be not condemned. Judgment and condemnation are the way of the Pharisee. Christianity is not anthropology; it is the revelation of the power and of the mercy of God. As the power of God is revealed in the heavens, so His mercy is displayed in the Church. And the Gospel of the Church is the Remission of Sin.

'Son, thy sins have been forgiven.'

'It is written that repentance and remission of sins should be preached unto all nations.'

'And the Lord said unto Saul, I am Jesus whom thou persecutest: I send thee unto the Gentiles to open their eyes that they may turn from darkness to light, from the power of Satan unto God, that they may receive remission of sins.'

'By Jesus Christ we have redemption by his Blood, namely, forgiveness of sins.'

In the Matthaean account of the Last Supper the Lord's words are thus recorded:

'This is my Blood of the Covenant which is being poured out for remission of sins.'

The Greek word which is variously translated 'remission' or 'forgiveness' in our English versions is ἄφεσις. And it is an interesting word because it has two meanings. It may be used for the cancelling of a debt, and in this sense it is used in St Matthew's form of the Lord's Prayer, 'Cancel us our debts', and the same meaning is presumed in St Luke's version, though he has the word 'sins' for debts. The meaning in both cases is clear.

Men cannot pay what they owe to God, and they run up an ever-increasing overdraft, which is blotted out and is continually cancelled by the mercy of God. This financial metaphor underlies the use of the noun or the verb in almost every case where it is used in the New Testament, and the correct translation is therefore 'forgiveness' or 'to forgive'. But there is another meaning of the word ἄφεσις which lurks behind its use at every point. It calls up the picture of a captive who, set free from a tyranny, gains his freedom, and should be translated 'release'.

'He hath sent me to proclaim release to the captives,
 and recovering of sight to the blind,
 to set at liberty them that are bruised.'

Here something more than forgiveness is meant. The Gospel of the Church is to proclaim forgiveness of sin, and freedom from its destructive power, a real purification, is suggested. But we have no English word capable of this double meaning, and disastrous consequences have followed from this disability. We have thought that our religion is powerless for purification, and has only to trumpet for the forgiveness of God, or on the other hand that forgiveness is but a lame and rather unnecessary adjunct to a righteousness actually possessed. And so we are tempted to say with the theological student in an endeavour to be scrupulously orthodox, 'We are justified by faith, but a few good works do not matter'. Or we secretly agree with the priggish John Evelyn when he wrote to his grandson: 'When a sin is dead, and an habit crucified, 'tis then pardoned.'

Can you again maintain a paradox? Can you explain

a No from a Yes, and a Yes from a No? and see the truth
in a contrast because it is a contrast without any attempt
at a synthesis?

Can you and I swallow our pride and stand naked
before God with nothing in our hands, with no claim
upon His justice, only requiring His mercy and asking
His forgiveness? Can we recognise that we are just part
of that busy world that crucified the Christ, and continues to do so, and then expect no demand: that just
when we stand thus humiliated not only are we forgiven, but purified, mightily purified, with the pride
burnt out of us, and the lusts of the flesh and the evil
imaginings of our heart scorched, so that the fruit of the
spirit is love, joy, peace, long-suffering, kindness, goodness, faithfulness, meekness, temperance; and that these
are not dreams in which we sometimes indulge, but they
walk before us concreted in the flesh and blood of the
man whom God has caught and twisted, and bent to
His will? There can be no boasting here, because what
is uppermost in the mind is the humiliation of it all,
and because the whole world of evil is still rampant and
alive in us.

There is the paradox, and there is no synthesis in this
world.

VIII. SIN AND THE LOVE OF GOD

And thus, after long wandering through the busyness of
human life as it is depicted in the sacred Scriptures
which have been written for our learning, we have
watched men driven from one seeming foothold to

another, ousted from the security of the wisdom of the world, forbidden to trust in the armies of princes or in their own good works, humiliated, ashamed, naked. But there, in the uttermost humiliation, at that dreadful moment the love of God is manifested, and on that foundation human life is once more built up, confident and secure.

This is the naked truth which you and I have to learn sooner or later, if we are to escape a cruel cynicism or an easy, unreal optimism. The Bible is struggling to say this. Throughout its pages, God is depicted as the lover of men, but His love is no mere benevolence. It is a grim story of war and famine and outlawry; Assyrian armies destroy nations, Babylonian princes drag whole peoples into captivity, rich men exploit the poor, and the poor are degraded, superstitious, licentious; they go a-whoring after this or that idolatrous worship, and the hearts of men walk after their eyes. But precisely where the utter futility of it all is clearly perceived, in men of flesh and blood, who share in the life of their people, who are themselves threatened with the complete downfall of everything in which they have trusted, there God makes Himself known, not in wrath and anger, but in forgiveness and in love, and in great power. On this rock the future is to be built if it is to be built securely: without it the greatest empires are built upon the sand, and the prosperous man cracks in his prosperity. This is what the prophets of Israel, what the psalmists, what the author of the Book of Job perceive, sometimes dimly, sometimes with brilliant clarity.

'The snares of death compassed me round about,
  and the pains of hell gat hold upon me.

I shall find trouble and heaviness,
and I will call upon the name of the Lord.
O Lord, I beseech thee, deliver my soul.
Gracious is the Lord and righteous;
  Yea, our God is merciful.' (Psalm cxvi. 3–5.)

'The floods are risen, O Lord,
The floods have lift up their voice,
The floods lift up their waves.
The waves of the sea are mighty
  And rage horribly.
But yet the Lord who dwelleth on high is mightier.'
        (Psalm xciii. 3, 4.)

'God is our hope and strength,
a very present help in trouble.
Therefore will we not fear,
though the earth be moved,
and though the hills be carried into the midst of the sea.
Be still then, and know that I am God.'
       (Psalm xlvi. 1, 2, 10.)

'Why do the heathen so furiously rage together,
and why do the people imagine a vain thing?
The kings of the earth stand up,
and the rulers take counsel together,
against the Lord, and against his Anointed....
Be wise now therefore, O ye kings.
Be learned, ye that are judges of the earth.
Serve the Lord in fear.' (Psalm ii. 1, 2, 10, 11.)

'The fear of the Lord is the beginning of wisdom.'
        (Proverbs i. 7.)

When we reach the New Testament we are transferred to no new plane; no new or hitherto unknown

God makes His appearance among men; no new truth, no new morality is revealed. To persuade men to separate the God of the Old Covenant from the God of the New Covenant is to resurrect the blasphemy of the greatest of all heretics—Marcion. The New Testament is simply the fulfilment of the Old Testament. There is found the same mingling of death and humiliation, the same passionate, fearless judgment of human life, and in this humiliation the same burning love of God for men. The mercy of God is indeed heightened, more penetrating, more widely effective, but only because in the Crucifixion of Jesus the humiliation reaches its utmost limit. This is the truth declared by our Lord in the words effectually uttered ever since at each Eucharist: *This is my Body which is given for you. This is my Blood which is shed for you. Take, eat. Drink ye all of this.* There is no escape from the inexorable law of the love of God.

Only in complete surrender, that is, in that surrender which is made not in theory but in the concrete happenings of real life, does the love of God burst forth. He is a jealous God, jealous of our affections, but unfathomably generous, when once He has men naked in His grasp.

'Jesus said, Verily I say unto you, There is no man that hath left house, or brethren, or sisters, or mother, or father, or children, or lands, for my sake, and for the Gospel's sake, but he shall receive a hundredfold now in this time, houses, and brethren, and sisters, and mothers, and children, and lands, with persecutions, and in the world to come eternal life.'

(St Mark x. 29 ff.)

And see too the reverse side of the picture, the picture of the world without God.

> 'As it came to pass in the days of Noah...they ate, they drank, they married, they were given in marriage. ...Likewise even as it came to pass in the days of Lot: they ate, they drank, they bought, they sold, they planted, they builded; but in the day that Lot went out from Sodom it rained fire and brimstone from heaven, and destroyed them all.... Whosoever shall seek to gain his life shall lose it: but whosoever shall lose his life shall preserve it.'
>
> (St Luke xvii. 26 ff.)

These sayings are oracles. In them the secret of life is condensed. They are creative aphorisms which penetrate truth, which explain the redemptive power of the Crucifixion, which call a new life into being and form character.

No wonder the disciples failed to understand what was meant. But as the time went on, and they were outcast and persecuted, and some of them had been killed, the Church recognised the truth, and it was perceived and accepted not merely by Jews, but by Gentiles, by harlots and by slaves. The background of this perception is neither the wisdom of the Schools, nor the security of wealth, nor the culture of the ancient world, but the rough and tumble of human life. Listen to St Paul: 'Where is the wise? where is the scribe? where is the disputer of this world? hath not God made foolish the wisdom of the world?...We preach Christ crucified....the power of God and the wisdom of God.'

'For thy sake we are killed all the day long; we were accounted as sheep for the slaughter.

Nay, in all these things we are more than conquerors, through him that loved us. For I am persuaded that neither death, nor life, nor angels, nor principalities, nor powers, nor things present, nor things to come, nor height, nor depth, nor any other creature shall be able to separate us from the love of God which is in Christ Jesus.'　　　　　　　(Romans viii. 36–39.)

But it is not until a generation, perhaps a generation and a half, had passed that we find a Christian able to sum up the whole meaning of this mingling of power and truth and humiliation in the words, *God is love*. Please do not misunderstand this: it is no casual, easy statement, nor is it spoken in a moment of emotional ecstasy. It is a sober, solid judgment, given in the light of the Crucifixion, uttered at a moment when the Christians were being severely persecuted, and when many, like Judas, had apostatised and, as St John says, gone out into the World, and surrendered their faith.

This is ultimately the meaning of the whole Bible, and it is the Gospel of the Church. And what a confidence it displays in the latent powers of men and women, that you and I are expected to bear this Gospel, to face up to it! Most of our generation are frightened of it when they once see it, and many clergy dare not proclaim it, and consequently we all tend to misunderstand the Bible and to misunderstand the Church. This is the great apostasy, when we substitute for the Gospel something less than the Gospel, because we do not believe either in ourselves or in our fellow men or women.

You, my brothers in Christ, who are to be ordained priests in the Church of England, will be ordained to preach this truth, and to take care that it is expressed in the worship which you will lead and conduct. But remember the limits of your ministry. You can compel no man to the truth. Nor is there any vicarious recognition of truth, and I beg you to respect the lives of others, and to beware how you meddle with them.

And we all, clergy and laity alike, have to learn to place first things first. We used, some of us, to think in terms of the reform of the Church, to suppose that a change here and a change there would bring the Church into greater harmony with the modern world. All this now seems very trivial. For the things which we believed in are found to be temporary, inadequate, and the Church remains the one hope of salvation, reformed or unreformed. It remains, because it is proclaiming truths which underlie our civilisation, which underlie our own busy lives, and which exist on a plane distinct from other truths or half-truths. And the scepticism with which we used to regard the Church is inevitably turned elsewhere.

III

THE VOCABULARY OF THE NEW TESTAMENT

THE LANGUAGE OF THE CHURCH

(1932–33)

I. THE LANGUAGE OF THE CHURCH

'Be ye not unwise, but understanding what the will of the Lord is.'   (Ephesians v. 17.)

The Church has a language: it possesses words and phrases: for example; Faith, Righteousness, Sin, Judgment, Flesh and Blood, Spirit, Death—Life, Darkness —Light, Wrath—Love, Evil—Good, the Devil—God. Upon the fabric of human life the Church embroiders its pictures and patterns by mingling in sharp contrasts the richly coloured threads of its language: or, putting the same thing in another way, upon the rich matter of men and women and things the Church stamps the form or impress of its words. But those metaphors are inadequate, for, in fact, the Church adds nothing either to the fabric or to the matter of human life: it does not, like some cosmopolitan organisation, seek to impose its will upon others for their good or for their destruction. For the fabric of human life has the picture and pattern already embroidered on it, and the matter is already stamped with form and impress. God has already woven both fabric and picture into one indissoluble whole; He has already stamped men and things with His image; and the Church does but, like some John the Baptist, point to what the world is. The Church does not manipulate or 'propagand': it bears witness, or rather, if it does juggle with human life and 'propagand' and manipulate, it becomes an object abhorrent both to God and to men.

The language of the Church is, then, no new language. The Church does not create its words any more than it creates its worship. It uses words which are common to all languages of all epochs, just as it uses worship familiar to all peoples of all times. The Church does not require of us that we should master a new vocabulary, but that we should apprehend the meaning of the commonest words in our language; it demands that we should not, at the critical moment, turn away from the meaning of words, but that we should wrestle with them and refuse to let them go. For from these common words, from 'life' and 'death', from 'good' and 'evil', from 'judgment' and 'mercy', there peers out at us from our quite normal, ordinary life, from the world of men and of things, a secret which concerns us and from which we cannot escape.

In spite of all that is said to the contrary, the Church is the enemy of all romanticism, if by 'romanticism' is meant a flight from the rough and tumble of things as they are into some dream world of our imaginings. The Church refuses to allow us to creep into some comfortable nook or to discover some 'cosy corner'; or, if we do take refuge in some such place, the Church soon reminds us that the place we have selected has a charge of dynamite under it, which may explode at any moment. Nor does the Church point to these explosions in order to pretend that she herself is the proper refuge of men, for the dynamite under the Church is most especially explosive. The Church has always a dagger at its heart, for it cannot long escape from its own theme, the theme which it is bound to proclaim—Christ Crucified. But we must not forget that even this theme is not something imposed by the Church upon the world, it is not some peculiar truth: it is rather that by which men are enabled to see clearly the tribulation which underlies their own selected place of security, whatever it may be. Every visible 'Christ' upon which they think they can stand, every '-ism' which we so passionately proclaim, every 'Movement' which we join, every truth *we* enunciate, every scepticism of which we are so proud when we have cynically detached ourselves from all 'Movements', all the pride of our aloofness and freedom from the superstition of every church and every conventicle, all our scepticism of science, not to mention our scepticism of theology—all these positions which we occupy pass like the Gospel story from Galilee to Jerusalem, from life to death.

But, though compelled by its theme to see and to announce this movement from Galilee to Jerusalem and to see it everywhere, the Church does not thereby make nonsense of human life; the Church is not so *unwise*, not so irrational, not so lacking in understanding what the will of the Lord is. For precisely at the point where it is confronted by crucifixion it proclaims resurrection. It proclaims Christ Risen, it announces a new heaven and a new earth, it announces consolation in tribulation. It makes sense of the nonsense, for, knowing that all visible things are done in parables, it proclaims the glory and righteousness of God, and it sees His glory and His righteousness made known where our glory and our righteousness manifestly break down.

Did we say that the Church makes sense of the nonsense? No, a thousand times no. *It* does not *make* sense, as though once again it were manipulating and propaganding: it simply sees that the sense is everywhere, because it sees, beyond human sin and inadequacy which is everywhere, not a void, not nonsense, but the fulness of the glory of God.

And so, though the Church seems so often to be moving towards cynicism and scepticism and irrationalism, at the supreme point, at Jerusalem where the Lord was crucified, the whole world—please notice, the *whole world*—comes back to us in all its vigorous energy, shining with the reflected glory of the God who made it and us, and with the reflected love of the God who has redeemed both it and us.

It is therefore precisely our failure, our sin, and finally our death which prevent us from supposing that we are sufficient of ourselves, and which make room for the glory of God.

The theme of the Church—Crucifixion-Resurrection—is therefore the song which is sung, whether it be recognised or not, by the whole world of men and things in their tribulation and in their merriment. This is the Gospel of the Church; the Gospel, because it is the Gospel—of God. There is no question here of bringing men within the sphere of the Truth, for they are already there. God is not the God of the Jews only, but of the Gentiles also, of the Anti-clericals and the Communists, of all the 'Movements' which tingle with resentment against the Church. He is also the God of the superior, detached person who, like Gallio, pins his faith neither on the Church nor on its opponents.

Yet, though the Church cannot bring men within the sphere of the Truth since they are already there, it can, if it be true to the theme by which its pride is destroyed, enable men to see the Truth in which men are standing. The Church can make sense of the pandemonium and the nonsense of the conflict between religion and irreligion; it can even make sense of the superior person who has removed himself from the conflict, by shewing that he too is a parable of the peace of God which passeth all understanding, and that he is a parable precisely when, at the last moment, he, too, is swept into the turmoil and finds that after all he has taken a side, and that peace and rest really do pass all understanding, because they are not found even in him.

Now, does all this sound difficult to you? Yes, assuredly it does. For though 'simplicity' is undoubtedly the mark of Divinity—God is One—yet we are not God: we are many—many opinions, many controversies, much disunion and disharmony. We can only hear the harmony of the simplicity of God in so far as it lies beyond the discord in which we are all irretrievably involved.

The whole modern cry for simplicity in religion is false, except in so far as it marks our longing for God. The Church cannot answer this cry directly without exalting some human philosophy or aesthetic feeling or programme or reform or revolution or conservatism and setting it upon the throne of God. But this is blasphemy, that blasphemy which is the greatest temptation of the Church as it is of all men: the temptation to fashion a God for ourselves and to fall down before the idol which we have made. At the moment of the Church's greatest tribulation and temptation and guilt, it is called back to proclaim Christ Crucified and to make room for the worship of the true and living God.

The Church and its Gospel do not, as so many people think, lie as outworn things behind our civilisation; they

are not relics of barbarism. They lie rather ahead of our
civilisation and of our lives, not as some extra, additional
knowledge which we may acquire, but, presuming the
achievements of men, their great and noble achievements, the Church speaks and can only speak when the
question is asked, Why should not so many great
achievements lead to universal permanent peace and
happiness and prosperity, why do they not lead to a
peace which we can altogether understand and enjoy;
why, in other words, in spite of all those pinnacles upon
which we stand and up which we have, with so much
difficulty, scrambled, do we still hear the sound of the
theme of death, why does the theory we have accepted
to explain human life still become so doubtful and
ambiguous when we really put our trust in it?

Only when this question is formulated can the Church
really speak. It utters its voice over the grave, not
merely of our bodies, but of all our pride and arrogance.
Until we have met the problem of all problems, the
Church can only be a thing to be loved or hated, a thing
to be learnt about or disregarded: it cannot be the answer
of God to the problem of sin and death. The Church can
sing the song of the redeemed only to those who know
that they are mortal, and that everything they can
touch and hear and see is mortal also.

You will have noticed that in announcing the Gospel
of the Church I have been pressed back again and again
to the language of the Church, which is the language of
men stamped with the Truth of God. And this gives my
subject for these two terms, a subject which we have
often come up against in the past, but which I too often

turned away from just when I should have persisted: I mean, the actual concrete words which form the foundation stones of the Church's language: Spirit, Love, Flesh and Blood, Hope, World, Death, Father, Wrath, Judgment. We cannot talk to Isaiah or Job, or Paul or John. We have only their words, and we ought to assume that the words they used made sense, at least to them. We ought to assume that their words are not counters to which we can assign any value we like, but that they are crying out at us, as though they had something to say which we ought to hear.

If the theme of the Church were just an additional bit of knowledge, it would be difficult to defend the existence of this Chapel in our midst, for it would then be an extra, voluntary subject taken up by some few who are for some reason or other temperamentally suited to it or interested in it.

If, on the other hand, the Church is saying something to us which we all are, if it is speaking to us of the relation between men—not *some* men, but *men*—and God, then we ought not to remove ourselves from the place where the Church utters, however feebly, its truth. And we ought to be careful lest we should expect the Church merely to frank our opinions, and to give it a miss in baulk if it does not. Indeed, if God be God and not man, we must expect to be somewhat uncomfortable in His Presence. The manifest impossibility of arranging services so that every one of you shall have what he wants is itself a parable of the offence and scandal that God is to us. What God wills is not identical with what we will. 'I set in Zion a rock of offence and a stone of stumbling', and we must always remember that it is not the failure of the Church which is the real trouble, but its far too great success in accommodating itself to the Spirit of the Age.

And therefore it is important that you should make some voluntary rule of life which carries with it the worship of God at least once on a Sunday, and that you should quite frankly recognise that, though the great truths of the Christian religion will be presented to you in the liturgy of the Church, they cannot be presented to you in such a way as to cause you no discomfort and no disturbance, and that for that very reason it is exceedingly easy to slip into carelessness about the honour which should be paid to God. For some it is particularly easy to search out some place where they will feel comfortable and at home, but in our relation to God that is precisely what we cannot have. We can only be comfortable and at home with some God who is, in fact, No-God.

II. 'THE WORLD'

'He was in the world, and the world was made by him, and the world knew him not.'

(St John i. 10.)

During these two winter terms I propose to take certain words which form the ground bass of the Church's language and to attempt their exposition.

In approaching the Church's language I would ask you to remember certain things by way of introduction.

First, words are not trivial things. To wrestle with the meanings of words is the road to the understanding of any subject: to be careless about them means a disastrous carelessness in the soul. And this is peculiarly the case with the Church's language. If the history of the Hebrew prophets and of Jesus and His Apostles is to be taken seriously at all, we must remember the quite simple fact that we cannot go and have tea with Isaiah or with St Paul and ask them what they meant, and perhaps indeed they could not tell us if we could do so. If we are to understand them, we can do so only by wrestling with the words they once spoke or wrote, and which have in part been preserved for us.

Secondly, we must assume that words do make sense, however much they may seem to us to make nonsense. That is to say, when the Church speaks, it is not uttering pure abracadabra, however much we may think it is. The vocabulary of the Church must not be treated by us as a series of counters which we can play with as we like, assigning to the words any meaning we like; this would simply be to play a game with the Church, and to write upon its face our ideas. That is fudge. And fudging with the Church is a far more serious matter than modern people are wont to suppose, for to fudge religion and make it represent your ego or mine probably means that we are going to fudge everywhere. The Church is the place where we have to learn to be honest, however disturbing this uprightness may be to our pride, because in the end and at the beginning and in the middle the theme of the Church is the relation between God and man, and to write our own names across the Name of God is idolatry. The Church speaks and must speak to us in words, and our honesty is tested by our attitude to these words.

Thirdly, when we do come face to face with the

Church's essential vocabulary, we are at once met by a rather surprising fact. The words are not elaborate words. They are, many of them, words of one syllable only: God, Man, Life, Death, Flesh, Blood, Sin, World, Light, Peace, Wrath, Lord, and so on. But here is the trap for the unwary. It is easy to speak these words, but only those who have been battered about can even begin to see what these words are talking about. These words are themselves subjected to terrible blows, tossed out of security into complete insecurity, and in that insecurity men have uttered them. In other words, when we dare to speak the words of the Church, we are in the presence of human life when it is most intense and most ambiguous, when it discovers that it has no solid ground under its feet. Confronted by the language of the Church you and I are confronted by a disturbing factor. And we must be prepared for this.

And now let us plunge *in medias res*, for generalisations are wearisome things, and may be found to be untrue.

The word 'World' clearly is a prime word of the Church. The Church and the World. The World in the Church. The World into which Christ came, the World which was in some unfathomable sense His, but which 'knew Him not'. The World which was created by God and lieth in darkness. The Prince of this World—meaning the Devil. The salvation of the World. I came not to judge the World. For judgment am I come into the World. Ye are the light of the World. We, when we were children (which we still are) were held in bondage under the rudiments of the World.

These phrases show at once how apparently chaotic

and contradictory are the things which are stamped upon the word 'World' in the language of the Church. If, for example, we ask whether the World is something which we are to accept and affirm or renounce and reject, we do not know how to answer the question. Nor can we escape the difficulty by saying that the chaos is simply due to pessimism or optimism in the various writers in the New Testament, for the contradictions jostle one another out of the mouth of the same writers almost in one breath. We cannot set Jesus against Paul, or the parables against the Passion narrative, or Victorian England against post-war disillusionment, or Resurrection against the Cross, or the Gospel against the Church, or the Creator against the Redeemer, since the point is that the theme is one theme and the contradiction is the theme and our New Testament writers use one word to express it. That word is κόσμος, translated into Latin by *mundus* and into English by *world*. Behind the Church's use of the word *world*, or *mundus*, or whatever other translation there may be, lies the Greek word κόσμος as it enters into the Church's vocabulary.

In modern English the word *cosmos* survives in a series of rather highbrow, semi-scientific, semi-philosophical, semi-ecclesiastical technical terms, such as cosmogony or cosmology, where it denotes some kind of scientific or philosophic analysis of the physical structure of the universe. Only in one word—and even then still rather technical—does it preserve a strict relationship with the popular usage of the word behind the New Testament, and that is the word 'cosmetics', denoting any material used for smoothing out wrinkles or other disfigurements of the human face. Adornment, orderliness, the beauty of regularity, these are the proper meanings attaching to the Greek verb κοσμεῖν, the root meaning of which is to arrange in order and so to equip or dress, especially of women. The noun κόσμος therefore implies good order, good behaviour, discipline, ornament or decoration (especially of women).

The link between the meaning 'good order' and the visible world is of course obvious. Regularity, for example, of the rising and setting sun, of the cycle of the seasons, of birth and death, is to the observer of the things which surround him and upon which he depends, their most characteristic feature. There is therefore no difficulty in seeing how the visible world of men and things was denoted by a word the primary meaning of which is orderliness. The word then enters the realm of Greek philosophy. But there is no reason to think that it was the philosophers who first called the visible world of men and things a κόσμος, an ordered whole.

The moment we take our New Testament into our hands we find the word κόσμος, meaning 'the world', used everywhere. To no New Testament author is the word not a prime and important word. But when we look at the manner in which they use the word we ought, I think, to be surprised. The thing is hardly believable. The word, which after all still means order, for κόσμος can in itself mean nothing else, is used throughout the New Testament to describe what our New Testament writers find to be disorder. The world, as they see it, is marked by disorder. The orderliness of the world is to them a matter of faith: what they see actually confronting them is disorderliness. And yet it never seems to cross their minds to try and find another word for the world. They just leave the word κόσμος with its glaring contradiction written all over it.

Take, for instance, the Parable of the Tares. When the Lord looks at a field of corn what, in fact, does He see? Just the golden corn waving in the soft summer breezes? No, not at all. There was the wheat, but lo, then appeared tares also. To the Lord this is the parable. The field is the world, is the κόσμος, as the word stands in St Matthew's Gospel.

When we pass on in the New Testament we find St Paul faced by two great optimistic attempts to reduce the visible world of men to a strict orderliness. The first is that of the Jew with his disciplined Church undertaking its mission, of which Paul himself had been a most convinced emissary: but he has felt the Jewish Church explode under his feet, for it crucified the Christ, and therefore showed itself, in spite of all its orderliness, to have rejected God.

The other orderliness which St Paul sees is the orderliness of the wisdom of the Greeks: but he has seen it to be unequal to the task of bringing the minds of men into a systematic order, and he pronounces the wisdom of the Greeks to be a wisdom of this world, for he finds the wise Greeks laughing at Christ and making Him foolishness.

In other words, our New Testament writers are honest enough not to be romanticised either by the prestige of the Jewish Church or by the wisdom of the Greeks, or by the apparent orderliness of Nature. In so far as there is visible order it is pointing towards an all-embracing invisible order which is human life in God and Nature as God's creation.

Now, we must not misunderstand the Church's contradictory meanings of the word κόσμος. There is here no irrationalism, no easy disillusionment, for these are just inverted forms of romanticism. What the Church presents to us is that the order to which the word κόσμος is pointing is the order of God the Creator and Redeemer of men, His Oneness, and our Oneness in Him. But, having said this, the Church at once says in the same breath that neither you nor I are in ourselves God and that what we see or do or think runs at some point or other to manifest incompleteness and disorder. For the honour of God we must recognise this, and we must not idealise ourselves and in so doing dethrone God. And so the word κόσμος is crossed, when we use it, by the whole fragmentariness of what we see, so that the glory of God is seen, not at the point where we are strong, but at the point where we know ourselves to be weak and in need of His mercy.

Is—and I think we must ask this question—is the language of the Church here cruel? Yes, at first sight it does seem to be so. We are, I suppose, all moving along some line. We all quite rightly think that the problems to which we are addressing ourselves are soluble problems; only so can we, in fact, bear witness to the glory of God not as chaos but as order, as the Creator of the world and its Saviour. Is it cruel, then, when the Church sees that the glory is God's, and that therefore we must not suppose that the final solution of our problems lies at *our* hands just round the corner, and that a few more years' science or theology or whatever it may be will land us all into the straight?

The real cruelty is surely to talk as though the final solution *did* lie just round the corner; cruel, not least because we should then be wholly surprised and knocked off our balance when we find the country getting perhaps rougher and not smoother. It is not the Church which is cruel, but the smooth-voiced propagandists of the modern world. It is the Church which ought to prepare us for this, and in fact does if we will only pay attention to it.

But it is not merely that the Church warns men against a manipulated and false security. It is concerned with truth, with our honesty. If you or I pay too much attention to modern propaganda gospels which promise a millennium round the corner in time and not in eternity we shall quite certainly falsify any work we are doing by making it square with some imposed, false *cosmo*politan doctrinaire propaganda dogmatism. And the real cruelty then may lie ahead. It may be that we shall not have to suffer, but the next generation, when our false work collapses, when we have not said that what we are doing is of this world, temporal, relative, is crossed by disorder, has ragged ends, or, in other words, bears witness by its relativity to the Absoluteness of God, Who alone is our Saviour.

III. 'THE NEIGHBOUR'

I am not surprised to hear of certain grumblings, no doubt friendly grumblings, that what I have said to you on the last two Sundays has been complicated and difficult to understand. The rebuke, which is of course not new, is not one to which I am callous, for I am quite aware that it is my responsibility to present to you the claim of the Church in such a way that it shall not sound mere abracadabra. At the same time you have to remember that the claim of the Church is not simple, for the very direct reason that human life, which is the theme of the Church, is not simple, at least as we are thrust into it. A simple Church is a Church divorced from the ambiguity of life, and therefore no Church at all.

As you now meet the Church in a College such as this, it is inevitable that it should make rather heavy demands upon you which in the last generation it did not. And this is, when you come to think of it, quite obvious.

First, for reasons which may seem to you good or bad, your attendance is voluntary. The claim of the Church upon you is not now supported by the discipline of the College, and that means that the issue is one upon which you have to make a decision, and if the decision is to be of any value it must not be capricious, for surely the chance that at any given moment you may feel like going to Chapel is no adequate alternative to the older compulsory system.

And secondly, the other great change is that there is no reason to think that in the future there will be a number of clerics on the staff of a college. In the old days in this College, even last year, if you came to Chapel on a week-day almost certainly the part of the laity would be taken by a second cleric. I mean quite simply the alternate verses of the Psalms or responses. That is now not normally the case, and a certain responsibility inevitably devolves upon you, should you enter the Chapel and find yourself one of a not very large number. There is no escape from the fact that the Church is making a very great demand upon its laity, a demand which ought, I think, to put you on your mettle. Whether the Church of England can present the truth of the Christian religion to our generation will depend very largely upon the extent to which well-disposed clergy and laity can co-operate in wrestling with the truth of the Church, and of this wrestling together the co-operation in the services of the Church is a parable.

> 'Thou shalt love the Lord thy God...
> and thy neighbour as thyself.
> But the lawyer said unto Jesus,
> Who is my neighbour?'

(St Luke x. 27, 29.)

In this passage there are two objects to the verb 'love', God and the neighbour, but the problem as it is set before us here lies in the meaning of the word '*neighbour*'. And this problem is presented to us in the Gospel narrative as an ultimate problem, for the passage begins with the question: 'Master, what shall I do to inherit eternal life?' It is in the context of eternal life that the New Testament and the Church utter the word 'neighbour'. But it is not only in the New Testament that the word 'neighbour' is quite fundamental; it is so also in the Old Testament, indeed the New Testament passages do but revolve round the great passages in the books of Leviticus and Deuteronomy, where the commandments of God are thrust upon the Hebrew people. 'Thou shalt not bear false witness against thy *neighbour*; thou shalt not covet thy neighbour's house, thou shalt not covet thy neighbour's wife, nor his manservant, nor his maidservant, nor his ox, nor his ass, nor anything that is his.' And then in the Book of Leviticus the whole command of God is summed up: 'Thou shalt love thy neighbour as thyself'. This is the passage which is picked out, not only in the Gospels, but also in the Pauline Epistles—e.g., Romans xiii. 8, 9—'He that loveth his neighbour hath fulfilled the law...for if there be any other commandment it is summed up in this word, namely, thou shalt love thy neighbour as thyself.' It is picked up also in the Epistle of James.

Now, I suppose you all react to this by thinking, yes, of course, 'love' is the theme of the Church, a theme which it persistently denies. Yes, but the attack on the Church, 'See how these Christians hate one another!' is far too simple, and it has disastrous implications, for when it is accepted it leads to the statement that all controversy, all quarrelling, all friction, all war, is contrary to what is called glibly the 'spirit' of the Christian religion. (I suppose the 'spirit' of the Christian religion means what the outsider has and the churchman has not.) But all this is far too easy, far too simple, and it results from a quite superficial and romantic use of the word 'love', without asking the previous question, What does the word 'neighbour' mean? let alone the other previous question, What does the word 'God' mean? for these are the proper objects of the word 'love'. In asking the meaning of the word 'neighbour', we are not of course playing with words, we are really asking what a neighbour in fact is.

But for the moment let us fix attention merely upon the word itself.

In the Church's language, the word 'neighbour' translates the Latin *proximus*; it translates the Greek πλήσιος; and behind this again lies the Hebrew root *raʿah*. None of these words are in themselves difficult words. They mean the man who is *near* to you, and 'neighbour' is a perfectly correct translation not only of the Latin, but also of the Greek and of the Hebrew. Not unnaturally, this word attracts to itself a number of parallel overlapping words, such as 'friend', so that we get the combination 'friends and neighbours'. Another overlapping word is 'companion'—'my companion and my own familiar friend'.

I need not press this. It is clear that the word 'neighbour' moves quite naturally from the merely physical juxtaposition of two people to a real union of interests and ideas, to a real communion of soul and spirit, so that the word 'neighbour' attracts to itself all the undertones of the word 'friend'.

And now comes the Biblical surprise, a parallel surprise to that which we met last week with the word 'Cosmos'. In the Biblical literature the word πλήσιος or 'neighbour' receives a shattering blow, for it takes to itself a whole series of over-tones which directly contradict the underlying meaning of 'friend'. The 'neighbour' in the Bible means the man who is not your friend, does not understand you, is outside your horizon, does not believe what you believe, is so much your opposite that at certain moments in the Bible the synonym for the word 'neighbour' is the Other. 'He that loveth "an Other" hath fulfilled the law.' 'If it be possible, as much as lieth in you, live peaceably.' Here is clearly no easy, obvious relation. Or again, in the Parable of

Dives and Lazarus, Dives' neighbour at his gate is described as at every point his opposite.

See how this sense of friction associated with the words 'neighbour' and 'friend' runs through the whole Biblical literature. It opens with the friction of the two brothers Cain and Abel, moves on through the stories of the patriarchs, settles down to the friction of Israel and its near neighbours the Philistines—the ἀλλόφυλοι, 'men of another race', of the Septuagint translation, and is a commonplace of the Psalms.

> 'My lovers and my friends stand aloof from me, and my neighbours stand afar off.'

Look at the paradox of that last statement!—Then the whole theme is summed up in the friends of Job, who are completely removed from any understanding whatever of the tribulation in which he stands.

The same paradox confronts us throughout the New Testament. Fellowship, Union, Love, Brotherhood, are words which clearly express the theme of the New Testament, but these words are never used easily. The friends of Jesus misunderstand Him. There is great friction between Paul and the earlier Apostles, which Paul is at no pains to disguise. Even Luke does not cover up the friction between Paul and Barnabas. The attitude of the New Testament writers to marriage and the family, for example, is shot through by the recognition that when they demand the unity of husband and wife, of parents and children, they are introducing no mere human demand, but a great, disturbing demand of God, so that the disciples say, 'If that be so, it is better not to marry'. The New Testament is no romantic idyll; it romanticises neither marriage, nor friendship, nor the family, nor even the Church. Everywhere it sees men confronted by Others, every 'I' confronted at every point by a 'Thou', and this friction is inescapeable. And yet in the midst of all this it goes on talking about Love and Unity and Brotherhood, goes on using the word 'neighbour' with its meaning 'near', not, please, because it thinks that we shall suddenly overcome the friction by engineering peace, but because it believes that God is One, and in Him, not in some human manipulation of human life, is the fulfilment of all this broken yearning for unity. But union with God is not a thing in this world, but a hope of eternity, a hope of the Day of the Lord, to which all the broken threads of human life are pointing.

Now, we must not misunderstand all this. There is here no denial of human love and friendship and brotherhood. David and Jonathan were friends, and so were Paul and Timothy. Nor have we the least reason to suppose that there were no happy families behind the New Testament writings. The point is that these relationships are human relationships; they are relative and insecure, not final and perfect, for the peace of God passeth all human understanding. There is in the New Testament no inverted romanticism of un-happiness and disillusionment such as meets us, for example, in the musical comedies of Mr Noel Coward, and in many modern novels. What the Church sees is friction, not unhappiness. Indeed it sees that human life must be lived in the quite fearless recognition of this insecurity of relationship between one man and another.

Now, once again may I ask you the question, Is the

Church cruel when it points this out, and demands that
men should see it and take account of it in all the arrange-
ments of this life? Surely the cruelty lies with those who
talk glibly about the brotherhood of man, and super-
ficially about peace, and romantically about marriage,
as though the disturbances in Church and State and
family were introduced into human life by a few evil-
minded men. This is the real cruelty. How will you face
up later to your married life, to your administration of
affairs, to your life in the Church, in fact to any real
part of your lives, if you are taught to think that your
'neighbour' will or ought to agree with you in all
points, will accept your solutions of his problems, will,
in fact, be the reflection of your image? Once we get
this stuff and nonsense into our heads we shall never be
able to live with any one or with any group of men. We
shall sulk when we are crossed, or run away from the
Others, for Others they are. We shall certainly remove
ourselves from the Church when we find it full of friction
and yet proclaiming the love of God. We shall then
never see that it is precisely this contradiction which is
the Truth of the Church, the Church humiliated and
brought into tribulation by the Gospel of the Glory of
God and of His Kingdom.

The Church, then, braces you to live your life among
neighbours, each one of whom confronts you as an
Other.

But now comes the point. Why does the Church make
sense, and not nonsense of all this? Why is the Church
thoroughly dissatisfied with a merely stoic attitude to
friction, why is the Church *not* sceptical though its
analysis of human life runs perilously close to the analysis

of the sceptic? Why does it insist on the contradiction which lies in the word 'neighbour'? Why does it feel uncomfortable when men talk so easily and glibly about the reunion of the Churches, or the peace of the world? Why does it fear the bandying about of the words 'Brotherhood' and 'Fellowship' as titles of every new society which good men found? These words are, of course, the very heart of the vocabulary of the Church, but wrenched out of the context in which they are disturbed words they sound perilously like sounding brass and a tinkling cymbal.

Let me just answer this question quite baldly. We shall have to come back to it on other Sundays.

The reason why we are bidden face up to our neighbour as someone who confronts us, stands opposite to us and not merely by our side, is that in him the Church sees the supreme parable of our relation to God. There can be no love of God which is not seen in and through our relation to our neighbour. There is no worship of God which does not take place in the context of our relation to our neighbours. What is visible is our neighbour, but God is invisible; we can only see Him as we learn to understand what our neighbour is. Sentimentalise our neighbour and we shall sentimentalise God. Clip off from our neighbour all that he is which differs from us, and we shall assuredly trim God to our own measure. Regard our neighbour as the reflection of ourselves instead of one who enters disturbingly into the world we have made for ourselves, and we shall certainly make of God an idol like unto us and we shall fall down and worship it. In that contradiction of nearness and remoteness which every neighbour is, we see the signpost which directs us towards the God Who is Other than we are, Who confronts our sin with His perfection and yet is our God, our Father, bound to us as Creator and Redeemer. And so, in the contradiction which lies in the word 'neighbour', the contradiction of near and far, of 'we' which is nevertheless 'I' and 'Thou', lies the manifestation of the Glory of God, and by our relation to our neighbour we are tested through Christ crucified in time and risen—in eternity.

This contradiction between time and eternity, between God and men as they are visibly, is the secret which is being set forth to us in the double meaning of the word κόσμος as it is used by the Church, though so often forgotten by us who call ourselves Church-men.

'He was in the world—and the world was made by Him—and the world knew Him not.'

That is the theme of the Church, and it is the theme of human life altogether.

IV. NOW—THEN; HERE—THERE

'*Now* it is high time to awake out of sleep.'
(Romans xiii. 11.)

'*Now* I know in part; but *then* shall I know even as I have been known.'   (I Corinthians xiii. 12.)

'Turn *now* every one from his evil way.'
(Jeremiah xxv. 5.)

Before saying something about these Biblical texts, I wish for a moment to come back to the subject of co-

operation between clergy and laity in the work of understanding the Christian religion, a co-operation of which
the co-operation in worship as, for example, in the quite
simple saying of responses, is a parable. There may be,
I think, some misunderstanding concerning this co-
operation in comprehending the themes of the Christian
religion. I did not mean that you all ought to become
theologians in the technical sense of the word. That
would be an unfair request for me to make of you. For
we must remember that the interpretation of the Bible
and of Christian doctrine is largely a technical matter,
and you are very much dependent upon those who have
devoted their lives to such subjects. Indeed, for this
very reason among others, you require a technically
trained clergy. I did not mean by co-operation that the
layman should endeavour to speak with authority on a
subject lying outside his genuine interest or capacity.
We suffer very badly at the present time from men who
with no proper knowledge suppose that they can rush
into print on theological matters without apparently
being aware where it is that the shoe is pinching. Nor,
I am sorry to say, are the clergy sufficiently careful of
recognising the limits of their own proper subject. It
was not to co-operation in ignorance that I wished to
urge you. We work together to an understanding of the
Christian religion when we all of us travel along the
road upon which we are each of us naturally moving
and along which we are qualified to move. God is the
end of every human road, if we will press along it to the
end, and if we will not stop and dream just at the
critical moment. We do not discover God by side-
stepping out of our natural road onto some other;

side-stepping is the essence of propaganda, not of that mission which sends men hurrying along the road upon which they have been set in a world of which God is both Creator and Redeemer.

You will co-operate in understanding the theme of the Church precisely as you genuinely face up to the obstacles which confront you on your own path, and refuse to pretend that they are not there. It may be that these obstacles are the theme of the Church. I refrain from illustrating this, but you will, I think, know what I mean.

Once again we are running into the Advent season, with its inexorable insistence that *now* is *the* time, that this very moment is confronted not by some re-organisation of human affairs which will soon be again dissolved in order to be again reformed and again dissolved, but by the dominion of God Himself, by His authority, by His Kingdom, by His veritable Advent or Coming.

I wonder if you are sufficiently aware how very difficult for us is this Biblical attitude to Time, or how challenging to our normal ways of thinking is the whole apprehension of Time which lies behind the Church's language, and which is summed up in those two monosyllables '*now*' and '*then*' set side by side, so that every moment in time is confronted, directly, urgently confronted, by the *then* of Eternity itself.

'Almighty God'—so runs the Collect for Advent Sunday—'give us grace that we may cast away the works of darkness *now* in the time of this mortal life'; and the Collect does but pick up the language of the whole prophetic Biblical literature, in which the Old and New Testaments move so naturally when they tend to revolve round the contrasts *now* and *then* or *here* and *there*. The problem of Space and Time is not a peculiar problem of the modern scientific world. It is just as much a problem familiar to those who are seriously attempting to make sense of the sacred books of the Church, though, of course, the Church is meeting the problem of Time in a different context from that in which the scientist meets it.

First, let me point out to you why it is that we find the language of the Church so strangely difficult. We have been brought up to think, consciously or unconsciously, in terms of evolution. No doubt we misunderstand and popularise the doctrine of evolution, but nevertheless we tend to think in terms of our popularised version of the doctrine. That is to say, we think of our own lives in terms of some form of gradual growth in moral stability, in knowledge, in the accumulation of experience. We hope to grow into maturity, into balance and poise, and we expect that we shall gradually attain to a rounded off, well-ordered personality. And if this does not quite work out as we had hoped, well, this growth to maturity will, we hope, take place in human society as a whole. It, at any rate, is surely, when considered broadly, moving towards balance and poise, to moral stability, to universal peace and prosperity, to a sound constitution; and our epoch, our individual lives, make sense when related to this whole process in which every moment in time is one in a great series, and is intelligible when thus thought of. The next stage in this, no doubt simplified, application of the doctrine of evolution is that we suppose that we know the goal to which all these moments are moving. We think we know the goal of time, as certainly as we know that if we board the 9.5 train we shall arrive at Liverpool Street. Knowing the goal, we are delighted to criticise those who are not moving in the 'right' direction. We set ourselves in opposition to those who are not in the van of progress. We name them reactionaries or obscurantists, and we see them very frequently still thinking the Church to be important, and so the Church becomes to us an obstacle to the progress of humanity. If, however, we are religious men, we tend to identify the Kingdom of God with our known goal of human progress, and then set the language and the reality of religion against the obstinate fact of the Church.

But we can do even more than this. Not only from the vantage point of our knowledge of the goal of human life can we divide our contemporaries into the sheep and the goats, but we can fit the whole panorama of history into our scheme of things. We can trace the progress of history as it moves towards its goal, and can deal out praise and blame according as this or that epoch, this or that man, has moved forward, ever so slightly, towards the city to which we think we are so much nearer than they were.

Now, it cannot surely be doubted that we do stand within the series of past, present, and future, that we are links in a chain, and that not only are we as individuals the product of an evolution, but that the epoch in which we live is intelligible to us only as the product of the past and the seed of the future. Indeed, our Christian language is drawn from the unextinguishable hope that the future will be better than the present and than the known records of the past. When our Biblical writers contrast what now is with what will be, they are moving within the concept of time and they are thinking of the movement of time towards a goal. Nor can we indeed be members of the Church without knowing that the Church belongs within the world of time and of history. We are taught this from our earliest days, when we read of the small primitive Church which was born out of Judaism and which expanded outwards from Jerusalem as a great mission to the world. As we grow older we are taught to see how its doctrine and its worship and ethics develop outwards in vast ramifications, how they encounter strange worlds of knowledge and experience, and how they assimilate new things and reform old things. We cannot really live at all if we do not share in this action and reaction, for it is our life and our work. It is, therefore, most important for us, as Christians, to recognise that neither the Bible nor the Church is unaware of the movement of history, of the links which bind the present both to the past and to the future. Are we then to reinterpret the whole Christian religion in erms of evolution and progress? Are we to spend our theological and religious energy in working towards the Kingdom of God as if it were a factor lying within the time series, either at a long distance away from us, or near at hand if we can persuade enough men of good will to set to work and usher in the Kingdom of God on earth? Are we to identify the Spirit of Christ with the modern spirit of progress? Or shall we, despairing of this, with a modern scepticism, be done with all idea of progress, and proclaim the world to be beyond our comprehending, and set out to eat and drink for to-morrow we die, to work with no real hope that our work can be more than a very insignificant thing?

It is when we have formulated the problem thus that the Bible and the Church begin to speak to us, and I doubt whether they can speak to us at all until we have been brought up against this question of all questions in some form or other, for the question concerns the meaning of human life, and that is the theme of the Bible and of the Church.

Once we tremble on the brink of real scepticism or on the brink of identifying the Kingdom of God with our ideas, the Church says to us certain things to which we ought to pay attention.

First, God is the Alpha and the Omega, the Beginning and the End. You will perhaps notice how strictly our Biblical writers hold to that truth. They have no adequate language to describe either the beginning or the end of anything. For this reason the beginning of the world and its ending are described in mythological language. The Bible begins with the first chapter of Genesis, which is neither history nor geology, and the creation of the world is not described thus merely because they have not sufficient knowledge, but because it is beyond our knowing. The Bible ends with the Apocalypse. We know neither end nor beginning. So is it with the beginning of our salvation and with its ending. The Evangelists bracket the Lord Jesus Christ with a miracle at the beginning and with Resurrection at the end. We Christians are, therefore, warned that the goal of human life and of human society is not a known fact on the plane of history from which we can start our thinking and divide men into sheep and goats according as they fit in or do not fit in to our pattern. God is the Judge, He is the End.

Secondly, the Church is vitally concerned with all that lies between Beginning and End. But it cannot see the observable world of men and of things primarily in terms of progress towards some far-off event, for the very simple reason that that would be to remove God from any near and intimate relation with men as they actually are here and now. Still less can the Church allow us to think of all that lies between Beginning and End as really nonsense. And so the Church dares to utter its great word 'Now', and it is spoken to men on whatever rung of the ladder of progress they may happen to stand: 'Now is the acceptable time, Now is the day of salvation.' Each moment of time is confronted by the glory of God, the 'Then' of the Biblical writers. Each moment of time is heavy with present significance and meaning, not so much because of its relation to some far-off event in time and in history, but because of its relation to the dominion of God. All our ideas and longings for righteousness and goodness and peace, all our yearning for mercy and charity, all our hope for some ultimate knowledge, all our desire to be forgiven what we have done wrong and that evil should be destroyed—all this is met *now* by the righteousness and goodness and peace and mercy and knowledge and wrath and love of God, in fact, by the glory of His Kingdom. Linked to that eternity each moment in time, each moment of our lives, becomes a significant moment, not because it is in itself eternity, but because it points to eternity and is fulfilled in it.

V. 'TRIBULATION'—'COMFORT'

'Blessed be God...who comforteth us in all our tribulation, that we may be able to comfort them which are in any trouble.'

(II Corinthians i. 3, 4.)

During last term I ventured to recall you to the Biblical language, to the words in which the Church dares to utter the Gospel of God. There is, of course, a contradiction here, a contradiction of which the Church is fully aware. We have to declare the glory of the ineffable, invisible God in words which have been formed to express visible or, at least, analysable things, and further it is *we* who have to speak these words, we who belong to the world as it is, to the present time, we who are flesh and blood, we who are men and not God. And yet, recognising, as the Church has always done, this double limitation, the limitation both of our language and of ourselves, we are pledged to utter the Word of God, we are pledged to share in or to conduct the worship of God, a worship which we all know to be far too human, far too inadequate, far too much mixed up with our pride of achievement, with our protests and irritations, but which, nevertheless, does, in spite of, nay, because of, these inadequacies, in very truth declare the glory of God, declare it because our Christian worship speaks so much of flesh and blood, of weakness, of the weakness which makes sense only if it be there, and there only, that the power of God, yes—*of God*, is manifested, revealed and made known.

And so it is that our Christian language is a disturbed

language; the words we use are, when fashioned to declare the glory of God, bent out of the straight, deflected, and sometimes actually reversed. Last term I illustrated this disturbance of the meaning of words by taking the Biblical use of the words 'World' and 'Neighbour'. Now we will take the pair of words 'Tribulation' —'Comfort'. They belong together in the Bible, which speaks much of tribulation, but never speaks of it, and indeed cannot speak of it, except in the context of a great, all-embracing consolation. So that, to generalise, we can say that the Bible speaks of consolation in tribulation, and indeed it speaks of nothing else. But we must ask—of what 'tribulation' is the Bible speaking here? And of what 'consolation' or comfort?

First, however, we must actually hear the Biblical juxtaposition as it is set forth by prophet, by wise man, by Apostle, by Evangelist and by the Lord Himself, and notice how this chorus of witness is taken up and repeated in our Prayer Book. If we do not hear this, we shall not be set the task of penetrating the theme of the Bible, and if we do not seize its theme we shall play all kinds of tricks and cruelties with our own lives and with the lives of our neighbours.

First of all, then, the words themselves.

Our English word 'Tribulation' as it is used in the English Bible simply reproduces the Latin of the great Vulgate translation which underlies the whole of Western Christendom. *Tribulatio* is the Latin word. Similarly 'comfort' and 'consolation' reproduce the Latin words *confortare*, *consolatio*, *consolator*, and the verb *consolari*. All these words are, of course, the best that Jerome and other translators could do to reproduce the Greek Bible,

which was the Bible used by the Christians in the first
and second centuries. Now the Greek word for tribulation in the Old and New Testament is θλῖψις and for
comfort or consolation is παράκλησις (παρακαλεῖν)
which comes down to us in the word 'Paraclete' used
for the Spirit in the Gospel of St John. It is here that
the story becomes strange and rather surprising. In
ordinary classical Greek, and apparently in the spoken
Greek of the first century, neither the word θλῖψις nor
the word παράκλησις is particularly significant. θλῖψις
means a rubbing or some kind of pressure. παράκλησις
means a calling for assistance or some kind of exhortation, as, for example, when Polybius says men fighting
for their homes and families require no exhortation
(παράκλησις), but mercenary soldiers do. But neither
of them is a common word.

It is clear, therefore, that somewhat trivial Greek
words were taken over, first to translate significant words
in the Hebrew of the Old Testament, and then by the
Christian Evangelists and Apostles to express the heart
of the Gospel of the Church. Both words, then, owe
their peculiar significance to the peculiar background
of the Church, to the Prophets of Israel and to the Lord
and His Apostles. We are therefore in the presence of
another illustration of the manner in which not only men
are being disturbed and knocked out of the straight, but
words also.

Now, listen to the actual use of the words at great
moments in the Biblical literature.

The book of Isaiah as it stands is, of course, not one
book but two books, recording the utterances of two
quite different prophets of Israel, to which other frag-

ments are attached. The second of these prophets opens
his mouth with ch. xl. of the Book of Isaiah. You ought
to think of this chapter, therefore, as the beginning of a
new prophecy.

Now then, listen to his words:

'Comfort ye, comfort ye my people, saith your God.
Speak ye comfortably to Jerusalem,
And cry unto her,.
That her warfare is accomplished,
That her iniquity is pardoned.'

Here, clearly, is the comfort or consolation *of God*,
announced by the Prophet to Israel in her great tribulation, in her warfare and in her iniquity.

The prophet returns to the theme in ch. li:

'I—the Lord—even I—am he that comforteth you:
Who art thou to be afraid of mortal men,
who shall be made as grass,
And forgettest the Lord thy maker?'

Here again the prophet speaks to men frightened by
the world as it is.

There is, however, running through the Old Testament the negative side to this confident proclamation of
the consolation—*of God*. So great is the tribulation or
distress or adversity or trouble or necessity—all these
are great Biblical words—that every human attempt to
alleviate it, every reformation, such as Isaiah's, every
bit of human kindness or charity, every human promise
of a 'good time coming', appears trivial, superficial,
almost a mockery, to men who require consolation
'*now*'—in their present distress. This is, of course, the

theme of the Book of Job, the theme also of that terrible, but most desperately Christian book—the Book of Ecclesiastes. The three very human friends of Job do set out very earnestly, and sometimes with real sympathy, to explain to Job why it is not unreasonable that he should be in such great distress, why he ought to bear it with courage and fortitude, and why he ought not to complain, until, and this is the point, maddened by this triviality, Job bursts out at them, at these good men:

> 'Then Job answered and said,
> I have heard many such things:
> Miserable, wearisome *comforters* are ye all.'
> (Job xvi. 1, 2.)

It is not until God Himself speaks that the complaint of Job is set at rest—and the whole point is that it is God Who speaks, for, after all, what God says is very much what Eliphaz, the wisest of Job's friends, had said all along.

The Prophet Jeremiah, like Job and the Psalmists, has the same horror of consolation which, when it is merely human, is by itself and in itself a mockery of the man in genuine distress. He, too, cries out to God:

> 'Thou art my hope in the day of trouble.'
> (Jeremiah xvii. 17.)

Or

> 'Hear the word of the Lord...
> I will turn their mourning into joy,
> and will comfort them,
> And make them rejoice from their suffering.'
> (Jeremiah xxxi. 10, 13.)

The same appears in the heart of the Law:

'When thou art in tribulation...
If thou turn to the Lord...
He will not forsake thee, neither destroy thee....'
(Deuteronomy iv. 30, 31.)

In the New Testament this whole theme becomes even more insistent, for the theme of tribulation becomes all-embracing and it is only in that vast situation that our New Testament writers dare to speak of consolation, but then they must utter it, for a divine necessity is laid upon them lest they and the Church with them sink to a trivial mockery like the Friends of Job, lest they, like the Pharisee and the Levite, pass by the man who is stripped and naked and half dead—on the other side; lest they should sink into human movements for reform of this or that kind and not dare to utter and proclaim the Gospel of God; please notice the New Testament emphasis, the Gospel *of God*.

It is as though the New Testament writers thrust men into tribulation. But they do not really do that, they only make it plain that in spite of all the wisdom of the Greeks, and the piety of the Pharisees, and the bubbling experience of Christians, like for example those at Corinth or in our modern 'Movements', all are nevertheless in the great tribulation, and that there is no good news which is adequate to meet this situation but the Word of God.

Listen now to St Paul:

'Blessed be God...who comforteth us in all our tribulation, that we may be able to comfort them which are in any trouble.' (II Corinthians i. 3, 4.)

Or again:

'Let us rejoice in hope of the glory of God.
And not only so, but let us rejoice in tribulations...
Knowing that tribulation worketh...hope:
And hope putteth not to shame.' (Romans v. 2–5.)

Or again:

'Now our Lord Jesus Christ and God our Father
which...gave us eternal comfort and good hope...
comfort your hearts and stablish you.'

Or Acts, where it is said that St Paul exhorted the
Christians to continue in the faith, explaining that
through many tribulations we must enter into the Kingdom of God (Acts xiv. 22); or the phrase in the Book of
Revelation where the elder explains who the great
multitude are:

'These are they which came out of great tribulation.'   (Revelation vii. 14.)

It ought not, therefore, to surprise us when we find
that, when the author of the Fourth Gospel comes, at
the end of the New Testament period, to say what
Christianity in fact is, he both says that 'in the world ye
shall have tribulation' (xvi. 33) and then asserts that
the Holy Spirit of God is the Comforter or Paraclete
(xiv–xvi).

But wait a minute, for we have almost missed the
point at which all our New Testament writers have seen
tribulation—the deepest tribulation met by consolation.
They have, of course, seen it in the Passion and Death
of Jesus, met by that tremendous statement 'But God
raised him from the dead'.

Between the Old Testament and the New, between the world as we see it and the Kingdom of God as the point at which both contrasted worlds meet, they see the figure of Christ crucified and risen, they see the consolation of God meeting the tribulation of human life, and they hear the words 'Come unto me all ye that labour and are heavy laden, and I will give you rest' (Matthew xi. 28).

Coming from all this Biblical language, we ought, I think, to be relieved that our English Prayer Book breaks the movement of our worship to remind us of its theme:

'Hear what comfortable words our Saviour Christ saith unto all that truly turn to him.'

Then follow the words which have just been quoted.

Now what is all this language talking about? At first sight, when set over against all the excitement with which we are surrounded, set over against all the propaganda movements of our day—religious propaganda as well as other kinds of propaganda—it all sounds very depressing. And for this reason many serious-minded men have turned away from the Bible and from the Church, and have sought elsewhere a peace which the Bible and the Church could not offer them. Men have turned to Communism, for example, as offering some more easily accessible rearrangement of human affairs which will take the place of the Kingdom of God; but it seems that they do but thereby thrust men into precisely that tribulation of which the Bible is speaking when it sees Jerusalem in ruins or the Christ crucified, or the converted Christian still assailed by manifold temptations. Or men, less seriously minded and less honest, do not turn away from the Bible and the Church, but make of them some gloriously happy thing, some lay religion, some happy fellowship, happy in the conviction that it possesses, indeed is, the Kingdom of God, that its printing press is the *Christian* press, that the reforms it advocates are the salvation of the world from war and unemployment and from human distress, in fact that they have a comfortable nook where tribulation is not. And Youth, thinking this is Christianity, finds its idealism satisfied in some religious or other Movement as it is not satisfied in the Church which is so tied to its old forms and its old ceremonies, in fact, though they are not honest enough to say so, because the Church is still daring to use the language of the Bible and still daring to be tied by it.

But all these Movements are not what they claim to be, for they break on the tribulation which the Church knows so well but so often hides up, on the tribulation that the Kingdom of God cometh not as a thing which can be analysed or seen or observed. This is the tribulation which the Church knows and which it has to proclaim. But it can proclaim it only because it dares also to proclaim that the God Who alone can provide consolation in this ultimate tribulation of men, is the one, true, living God—Creator and Redeemer of men.

VI. THE WEAK AND THE STRONG

'We exhort you, brethren, warn them that are unruly, encourage the fainthearted, support the weak, be longsuffering towards all.'

(I Thessalonians v. 14.)

The Church is extremely sensitive towards the poor and the weak, to the maimed, the halt, the blind, to everything that is summed up in the one word 'Lazarus'. Nor is the Church afraid of the implications of this sensitiveness. The Church is unsympathetic, extremely unsympathetic, towards the rich and the strong, towards the powerful, the mighty, the proud, towards the Pharisees, in fact towards everything that is summed up in the one word 'Dives'.

Nor is this quite logical exercise of the Church's natural sympathy and natural distaste unintelligible. Did not Christianity come to us from the Jews? from the extreme weakness of the ancient Hebrews, from their uncultured poverty, from their isolation in the midst of Egypt and Assyria and Babylon and Greece and Rome, from a people who were strangers and pilgrims, from a nation which was regarded by the surrounding nations as having no form or comeliness, no beauty that they should desire him? Did not the great and powerful nations despise Israel, from whom the Christian Church has been born? Did they not, as the Prophet says, esteem him stricken, afflicted, wounded, bruised, chastised? This is the peculiar background of the Church, a background indeed gathered together and summed up in the figure of Jesus, persecuted and done to death by the strong; in the story of Jesus, the Son of Man, who, unlike the birds, unlike the foxes, had no nest, no hole in which he could lie down and rest—comfortably. Jerusalem, not Rome, is the place where the word of the Lord 'roared', as the Prophet wrote. From Zion the deliverer is come, as St Paul well knew. Think what that means, and do you wonder that the Church is sensitive to the claims of the weak and of the poor, or that it regards with real horror the strong and the rich?

It is not, then, surprising that the vast movements of our own day which spring from the earnest desire to raise the status of the poor and to care for the weak, for the diseased, for the feeble-minded, for the children, should cry out to the Church for support, should claim the Church's clear and direct sanction, should claim indeed the sanction of God Himself. And is it in the least surprising that the Church should have answered this appeal, should have indeed been in the forefront in awakening this social sense, in supporting hospitals, in building schools for the poor, in providing from its own members devoted men and women who have consecrated their whole lives to the service of the weak? Is it surprising that the conscience of the Church is outraged by the thought and memory of war in which the sufferings of the poor are accentuated, inevitably accentuated, and that the word 'peace' evokes a longing and yearning which cannot be permitted to evaporate in mere sentiment, but must be translated into action?

In this whole situation, moreover, is it surprising that, as we read our Bibles, we should find the direct exhortations to loving-kindness, to charity, to longsuffering at once intelligible and unmistakable? Do they not give us a perfectly clear line of action? Can there be any doubt whatever what action is demanded of us by God through Christ? Can we endure for one moment the quibbling of theologians or the embarrassment of the Church when it is faced by so clear a call? Can we endure for one moment the hesitation of any single Christian? Must we not set Christ over against the Church, over against Christendom, if the Church or Christendom pauses for an instant before it obeys the clarion call of the poor and of the weak? Let us not be in any doubt here. Lazarus and the man fallen among thieves must be the only concern of the Church. A Church which passes by on the other side is no Church of Christ; and the man who leaves Lazarus uncared for at his gate is no Christian. We must permit no quibbling, no embarrassment, no shivering on the brink of Christian Charity.

Yes, of course, but if Lazarus is the point to which the Church moves, if we see clearly the Good Samaritan crossing the road towards the place where the man fallen among thieves lies stripped and naked and half dead, it is surely quite obvious that we must know who Lazarus is, and where is the place where that man lies half dead. We must ask the question: Who are the poor? Who are the weak? Who are these to whom the Church ministers and must minister?

Once formulate this as a question, and it is the question with which St Paul is always wrestling, in all his Epistles. And it is a question which admits of no simple, obvious answer. This is the question which compels St Paul to write all those heavy eleven chapters of the Epistle to the Romans before he can, without the possibility of being gravely misunderstood, write the simple exhortations contained in the last four chapters. This is the question which causes him to write in the famous thirteenth chapter of the Epistle to the Corinthians the haunting words, 'though I give all my goods to feed the poor and though I give my body to be burned, and have not charity, it profiteth me nothing'. That is to say, this is the question which compels St Paul to set the theme of the Church, Charity, over against and in contrast with the whole heroism of human good works, and which makes him halt before them and wonder whether they be not sounding brass and a tinkling cymbal. This is the question which drives him to add to his exhortation to the Thessalonian Christians to support the weak, that they should be 'longsuffering towards all men', lest they should understand by 'the weak' a particular, concrete, detachable number of visible men and women, some 7000 in Israel, some one-and-three-quarter million in this country.

And so we encounter the two pairs of Biblical words, the Rich and the Poor, the Strong and the Weak, as a problem.

I need not on this occasion bother you by asking you to follow me in tracking these words back through the Latin and Greek to their Hebrew originals. We are confronted here by a problem in which the modern world is sufficient to provide the interpretation of our Christian language. For the Bible is set both in the ancient world and in our world, and the preacher stands always before the choice of drawing out old things or new things to interpret the theme of the Church, for the old and the new are equally pregnant with the secret of God. The poor are with us always, that is to say they are a permanent witness to what poverty and weakness really are.

I have a fear lest we Christians have gone materialist, and that we are nowhere in so grave a danger of materialism as at the moment when we utter the word 'poor' or 'weak', and that we are in this danger despite the phrase which meets us at the beginning of the Sermon on the Mount, the 'poor in spirit', a phrase introduced for the express purpose of preventing us from thinking of the poor or of the weak merely in terms of lack of money, or lack of robust physical health.

Will you question yourselves, each one of you, as to what you do in fact mean when you say 'a poor man'? Do you think at all in this context of the poverty of the man holding some great position in Church or State, but, whatever his income may happen to be, weighed down by responsibility and aware of how little he can, in fact, effect? Do you ever think in this context of the poverty of the Tory landowner struggling to keep together the heritage he has received from his father for the benefit not merely of himself or of his children, but, as he supposes, for the good of the village in which he has been brought up? Does it ever cross your mind to think in this connection, in the connection of the word 'poverty', of the French statesman who is responsible that France should not in the next generation be left wholly unprotected? Do you ever think in this connection of the officials at the War Office, who, fully aware of the horror of war, dare not behave as though peace were already assured? Do you ever think in this connection of the men, whatever their incomes may be, who perceive that there is truth precisely in what men and women are everywhere decrying, truth in what for example Galsworthy and the most applauded modern novelists have so bitterly attacked and caricatured, and yet are unable to persuade men to take seriously what they see? Are you quite certain that those whom you call the strong are not in fact the weak? Human life is strangely kaleidoscopic. The strong at one moment are the weak at another. The poor are not a fixed, easily recognisable quantity of men and women.

But please do not misunderstand this. I am not for one moment attempting to switch your recognition of what poverty is from one set of men who are physically poor to another set of men who may be suffering from a poverty of spirit, from a sense of oppression which is not so easily recognisable. I am only asking you as men of the world not to narrow your sympathies, but to widen them out, and to recognise that Lazarus is a more complicated figure than we are wont to allow.

In all this we have still reached no further than the threshold of what the Church means by Charity, of that embarrassment which faces the Church when it thinks of the poor or of the weak.

The Church sees men and women in the light of the righteousness and glory of God; His brightness and His holiness are the theme of the Church. Once the Church sees and knows and speaks, it is inevitable that the gulf should open out between the righteousness of men as we see and know it, and the righteousness of God; it is inevitable that, brought into His presence, all men should be shewn to be weak and poor, to stand in need of His mercy. It is from this situation that Christian Charity is born, and it is all-embracing. The Church bids us see Lazarus in Dives, to see the man who fell among thieves —dare we say it?—in the priest and the Levite, to see the Gentiles, in all the wealth of their culture, standing as the poor before the incomprehensible love of God.

This is the theme of all those long, dreadful early chapters of the Epistle to the Romans.

But we must not stop here, lest we be paralysed. When, guided by the Church, we have seen Lazarus everywhere, we must return to the quite concrete Lazarus who is our particular neighbour, the individual at our gates, the man whose spirit is distressed or whose body is crippled, and we must support the weak. But when we have said *we* must support the weak, we must remember that we can only do this, as Christians, as a sign and a witness, as a parable of the love of God which alone rescues our action, or the action of others towards us, from grating on our ears like sounding brass or a tinkling cymbal. Humanitarianism is neither the Alpha nor the Omega of the Christian religion, but, even in its crudest and most material form, it is the necessary parable of God, the Lover of men, Who is alone both Alpha and Omega.

VII. 'FLESH' AND 'BLOOD'

'Blessed art thou, Simon Bar-Jonah: for flesh and blood hath not revealed it unto thee, but my Father which is in heaven.'   (St Matthew xvi. 17.)

We come now to the phrase in which the theme of the Christian religion seems to verge upon the ridiculous: I mean the words 'flesh and blood'. And yet these are the words by which the Christian religion clearly stands or falls, for Christianity stands or falls at the point where it seems to become banal, and where it does in fact become a scandal to the mature, solid common sense of the intelligent man, aye of the intelligent and religiously-minded man: that is to say, it becomes a scandal at the point where you and I are actually standing.

The phrase 'flesh and blood', with its variant 'body and blood', has haunted the Church throughout its history. Every controversy in which the Church has engaged itself has become sooner or later a controversy about these words. On them the Church has broken into fragments; on them it still goes apart into its various nooks and corners. Everybody is on edge when, in the heart of a religion which claims to be the spiritual religion, they are confronted by these terrible words 'flesh and blood': everybody, even the most pious Christian, receives a jolt when he recognises that at the most sacred moment of Christian worship he is brought tumbling down to earth with the words 'body' (flesh) and 'blood'. Nor is it the Catholic-minded man alone who is hurt by this language. It confronts the Protestant also. 'Grant us therefore, gracious Lord, so to eat the flesh of Thy dear Son and to drink His blood'—this is all in a prayer added to the Liturgy at the Reformation.

With modern controversies I am not for the moment concerned; what I want to shew you is that it is not merely we moderns who are brought up short. The New Testament itself is fully aware of the scandal of its language. When the author of St John's Gospel reaches the words 'flesh and blood', he first declares that they are the very truth, for he represents the Lord as saying to the crowd 'except ye eat the flesh of the Son of man and drink his blood, ye have not life in yourselves', words which are then repeated more precisely, 'he that eateth my flesh and drinketh my blood hath eternal life, and I will raise him up at the last day'. The author of the Gospel is fully aware that he has recorded an outrageous contradiction in thus declaring eternal life to depend upon a relation to the flesh and blood of Jesus, the Son of Man, because, with fearless honesty, he not only asserts that the Jews regarded the language as ridiculous ('How can this man give us his flesh to eat?'), but also that many of the disciples, when they heard this, went away and ceased to be disciples of Jesus, saying 'This is a hard (outrageous) saying, who can hear it?' And then the author, and this is surely the surprise of the narrative, dares to say *in this context*: 'The flesh profiteth nothing.'

If we take it, as I think we must, that this whole passage was written at the very end of the first century or at the beginning of the second, that is at the end of the New Testament period, we know from the letter of St Ignatius to the Smyrnaeans that many Christians were refusing to assemble with other Christians precisely because the Church could not rid itself of this language, and the 'spiritually-minded' men were shocked at it, and refused, as St Ignatius says, to share the Eucharist with their brethren. Like the author of the Fourth Gospel, St Ignatius sees in such 'spirituality' a denial of the Christian religion, a denial of the 'Passion of the Lord'—this is his phrase.

It is then clear that when we are shocked by our Christian language we have behind us a host of others reaching back to the end of the first century who have been shocked in like manner.

But are we not bound to push the problem yet further back?

St Paul finds the Corinthian Christians meeting together for a happy kind of religious fellowship, which incidentally is not quite so magnificent as they think it is, but that is not the point. The point is that St Paul, just like St John, brings them sharp up against the words which alone can make their fellowship Christian, and the words are 'body and blood'. Unless they discern the Lord's 'body' their religious eating and drinking is not only unworthy, but it is for the worse; in other words they become worse men than they were before. And then, with a supreme contradiction, he, just like the author of the Fourth Gospel, goes on to say two chapters afterwards, 'Flesh and blood cannot inherit the kingdom of God'.

We cannot get over the difficulty, as we should perhaps like to do, by imagining that Paul and John invented the terrible phrase, or that they have borrowed it from contemporary mystery religions. The words not only stand in the earliest Gospel, that of St Mark, but they occur there with precisely the same tension as elsewhere in the New Testament. At the supreme moment before His death, the Lord not only speaks of His body and blood, but rivets the words upon His disciples by making them eat and drink in the context of these very words; and yet the whole positive episode, the Lord's positive words and His positive actions, run to a great negative, for He adds, 'I will not drink of the fruit of the vine until that day that I drink it new in the Kingdom of God' (Matthew adds, 'until I drink it new *with you*'): that is to say, the whole language about 'body and blood' is met by the phrase 'Kingdom of God' and by 'the Day of the Lord'. The disciples, of course, do not understand, for the Marcan narrative goes on and on inexorably underlining this inability to make anything of the whole situation, until, without any sentiment, Mark just says that they all forsook Him and fled.

What I want you to see from all this is that the words 'body' (flesh) and 'blood' not only lie behind our New Testament, not only express the tension of the Christian religion at its supreme point, but that they are very difficult words.

Can we do anything, not indeed to ease the difficulty, but to shew where the difficulty is really lying? I think we can.

The Greek words for flesh (or body) and blood are σάρξ, σῶμα, αἷμα. They are translated into Latin by *caro, corpus, sanguis*. The Church's word 'incarnation' is formed from *caro, carnis*, and behind it, of course, lies the Greek word σάρξ, which occurs in the Prologue to the

Fourth Gospel, 'The Word became flesh', or σάρξ, or *caro*.

This playing with Greek or Latin or English words may be very interesting, but it does not really help our understanding, for the words in English or Greek or Latin present no difficulty. 'Flesh' means just flesh, and 'blood' means blood, in English or in Latin or in Greek, and 'flesh and blood' does mean, yes, flesh and blood. It is not until you turn the phrase into the Hebrew that it becomes really interesting, not until you recognise that flesh and blood, *caro et sanguis*, σὰρξ καὶ αἷμα, are all translations which ultimately run back to the Hebrew or Aramaic phrase '*Basar we dam*'.

The phrase 'flesh and blood' in Hebrew and Aramaic (i.e. the spoken language of Palestine in the first century) meant a man, or men, and very particularly men in distinction from God; men, their thoughts and actions as distinguished from the thoughts and actions of God. The phrase defines human, analysable opinions and experiences and human visible and analysable behaviour as finite and temporal, as relative, as opposed to the infinite and eternal truth and righteousness of God. The phrase is therefore far more all-embracing than what is normally denoted by the two words *flesh* and *blood*. Let me illustrate the use of the words:

The Rabbi John, son of Zacchaeus, who died in the year 80 and was therefore a contemporary of most of our New Testament authors, said:

'If I am brought before a king of flesh and blood, should he be wroth with me and cause me to be bound with chains and put to death, his wrath is a temporal wrath, his chains are not eternal chains, nor is the death which he orders an eternal death. If, however, I am brought before the King of Kings—blessed be He—His wrath is the wrath of eternity, His chains are eternal chains, and the death which He orders is everlasting.'

But we need not really search among the sayings of obscure and forgotten Rabbis, for our Lord's words to Peter are in this connection perfectly clear. When Peter recognises Him as the Christ, our Lord's comment is: 'Blessed art thou, Simon Bar-Jonah, for flesh and blood hath not revealed it unto thee, but my Father which is in heaven.' Notice the sequence of the language—not flesh and blood, not men, *but*—God.

I take it that this piece of pure verbal interpretation must be hung onto when we come to interpret all these other New Testament passages in which the phrase *flesh* (or body) and *blood* occurs, especially since it tends to occur in close association with the parallel phrase 'Son of Man': 'Unless ye eat the *flesh* of the *Son of man* and drink his *blood*, ye have no life in you.'

Now, can we leap to the meaning of our Christian language? Can you see what this terrible and inexorable insistence of the Christian religion is really saying? Surely it is, at any rate formally, not as difficult as we have been led to suppose. By our Christian language, by the express doctrine of the Church and by its worship, we are being thrust into the whole relativity of human life, into the life where men are men and not God, where their ideas and notions are not the absolute Truth of God, where at best men speak in parables, and where their actions are not the righteousness of God, where, in fact, life passes to death, and where human visible progress is found to be not a straight road which runs unbroken into eternity or into the Kingdom of God, where we are compelled to recognise that God is God and men are men, and that there is no mixing of humanity and Divinity, no encircling of men with a Divine halo, no depressing of Divinity into an incomplete human shape or form. Into this realm of death the Lord passes with eyes wide open, with inexorable purpose, and into this realm He draws His disciples with Him.—Did we say *draws* His disciples? No, as men they are already passing thither, and He does but endeavour to make them see what He sees, and to force them to discard for ever the illusion that the Kingdom of God can be simply identified with some relative thing in this world, not even with His own miracles of healing, or with His magnificent ethical teaching.

Oh, yes, we can say all this, and not find the interpretation of the New Testament difficult; its meaning is clear enough. But can we live as the Church demands that we should live? Can we, as our Lord and His Apostles dared to say, can we eat the flesh of the Son of Man and drink His blood? Can we really live as though we were men and not God?

No, assuredly we cannot, if the Gospel of the Church be no more than a pseudo-gospel of death and of relativity, in fact of ultimate scepticism. Nor does the New Testament ever proclaim so barren a doctrine. Indeed, it could not insist so strongly that men are men, did not it see so clearly that at the point where men are found to be men, there, not only God is seen....*

* [The last page of this MS. is missing.—ED.]

VIII. 'SPIRIT'

'Quench not the Spirit. Despise not prophesyings.
Prove all things; hold fast that which is good.'
(I Thessalonians v. 19–21.)

With what word or phrase shall we conclude this selection of words from our specifically Christian language? Suppose we say that Ἀγάπη—Charity—Love—is the final Biblical, Christian word. We should then, of course, make no mistake, for did not our Lord Himself gather up His whole teaching in this one word: 'Thou shalt *love* the Lord thy God with all thy heart and with all thy soul and with all thy mind and with all thy strength'? Did not St Paul, echoing his Master's judgment, twice recall his readers to this final truth? 'Therefore', he writes to the Romans, 'Love is the fulfilling of the law': and, having led the Corinthians to the three great Christian words, Faith, Hope, and Love, he concludes by pronouncing that the greatest of these is Love (Charity, *caritas*). And did not St John, writing at the very end of the New Testament period, and in the midst of great tribulation and controversy, sum up the whole meaning of Christianity in the one final truth that God is Love and in the one final moral demand, 'My little children, love one another'?

Or shall we not be equally safe if we say that the final Christian word is 'Father' with its inevitable rider 'Son'? We need not surely spend our energy in proving that 'Father—Son' is the one final goal to which our whole religion moves. Do we not indeed know that the emphasis in our worship of God is a right emphasis when we begin at the step of the altar with a quiet 'Our Father, which art in heaven', and when, at the point where we have entered the Upper Room with the disciples of Jesus and have shared with them the Master's Body and Blood, we dare with great boldness this time to sing, and to sing joyfully, the words 'Our Father, which art in heaven', and do we not thereby proclaim that all men are the sons of God, however little they may recognise what they are? Have not we Christians at that moment seen and perceived and uttered the final truth?

Or shall we not be equally right if we say that the final truth is summed up in the phrase 'the Kingdom of God'? For does not the whole concrete visible world of men and of things make sense if it be seen, not as existing in itself, but as related to the invisible Dominion and Sovereignty of God? Is not this the very kernel of the concrete life and of the audible teaching of Jesus? do they not make nonsense if they be treated as relative things existing in their own right and be not related to the Kingdom of God? Indeed, did not the Lord Himself see His flesh and blood, His visible history, trembling on the brink, moving on the frontier, of that Kingdom which is nigh at hand, aye, even in your midst? And if we have seen the Dominion of God there, does it not, like the Love of God, press upon every moment of time and upon every temporal place, whether men do or do not perceive it?

Yes, all these are, in very truth, final Christian words, words which we must hold fast, beholding their form, giving shape and meaning and significance to their undisciplined matter: 'Hold fast, Timothy, the form of sound words which thou hast heard.'

But there is another final Christian word, a word so dangerous that, for fear of misunderstanding, we may be tempted to banish it from our vocabulary; I mean the word 'Spirit', 'the Holy Spirit', 'the Holy Spirit of God', 'Pentecost'. Was not the Lord moved and led by the Spirit? Was He not baptised, and does He not baptise men with the Holy Spirit and with fire? Were not His Apostles led by the Spirit, and did not the Spirit burst out upon those who believed through their preaching? Does not St Paul name the Christians spiritual, and does not St John end the record of the teaching of Jesus with the promise of the Spirit, the Comforter, the Paraclete, who is the Spirit of Truth? Is not the Christian religion the worship of God in Spirit and in Truth?

What, then, with all this language behind us, should be our attitude to all those '*spiritual*'—notice the occurrence of the word here—movements which bubble up in our midst, in the Church or without it, or in some strangely loose connection with it? What should be our relation to those sudden exaltations of *spirit*—notice again the occurrence of the word—which meet us in others or which meet us sometimes even in our own experience? What is to be our attitude to that romanticism which sometimes penetrates even the hearts of those who have seen most clearly the grim truth which the Christian religion is proclaiming when it says—'Christ Crucified'? Must we only weep with them that weep, must we not also rejoice with them that do rejoice? Must we not pipe a melody and clap our hands and eat and drink and be merry even though we know, like the epicureans of old, that to-morrow we die?

I have been compelled, in following the Christian

language, to say hard things, things which I know hurt some of you, about religious movements. This was necessary, because I wished to warn you against some crude and final identification of the operation of the Holy Spirit of God with some exaltations of your spirits. I have reminded you that to the Church has been entrusted the responsibility of checking human idolatrous illusions whereby men declare that their ego, their spirits, are the Holy Spirit of God, or that their society is the Kingdom of God, or that their very human principles are the ultimate Truth of God, or that their far too human exhibitions of affection are the love of God which passeth all understanding. I have also reminded you that the responsibility with which the Church has been entrusted in the world of men as a whole must be exercised by theology in the heart of every university and in every place of education. Theologians have long since discovered that even this most perfect and rounded-off system, even their most penetrating analysis of the Scriptures, even their most brilliant exposition of the Gospel, remains a relative human knowledge. Themselves broken upon the Truth of God, theologians are responsible to protect all newer roads of knowledge from the blasphemy for which theology has itself been punished and by which it has been so deeply scarred. The Church and theology know that they can only sing the song of the glory of God over their own graves and at the place where they have died. This is the secret of the Church; and can you wonder that those who know this secret tremble when they see scientists, economists, psychologists, Hitlerites, leaders of the Group Movement, Communists, and all those many other confident advisers of men marching with flags flying into the abyss where the Church has already stumbled and fallen?—can you wonder that the Church lifts up its voice and utters its tired, weary warning against human ὕβρις, arrogance?

And yet it is precisely at this point that the Church encounters its most subtle danger, and we are, as Churchmen, in most grave danger of the even more subtle menace of inverted arrogance—the arrogance of detached aloofness from the rough and tumble of human optimism and exaltation, in fact from the world of religion and reform and of romantic idealism.

How well St Paul knew this danger—and escaped it—but only by a hair's breadth. Did he not, with his clear eye, see quite clearly the relativity of all human experience, did he not, for that very reason, refuse to boast in his own spiritual experiences, did he not warn the Corinthians against the pride of their spiritual knowledge, did he not tremble when he heard of their speaking with tongues and of their prophesyings and of their determination to eat nothing but vegetables, in fact of their exalted asceticism? But did he ever, for that reason, cease from affection towards these little ones in Christ? Did he ever ridicule their heroism, pour scorn on their labour of love, or laugh at their work of faith and their endurance in hope? The Gospel which he proclaimed, though it never permitted him to boast except in his weakness, did not make him an aloof, critical, scornful person, proud in his lack of pride, boastful of his detachment from all exaltation of spirit. Indeed, did he not prophesy with the best of them; did he too not speak with tongues; could he not say, when pushed against his will to declare himself, that he had been exalted into the third heaven and had heard unspeakable things which it is not lawful for a man to utter? And so it is that we find in his Epistles a strange turning about of exhortation, for though he is a man out of whose being all illusions have been burnt, yet human sympathy has not been crushed in him, and he can, therefore, end the First Epistle to the Thessalonians with the words: 'Quench not the spirit, despise not prophesyings'. He does not, of course, mean quench not the Holy Spirit, as though it were possible to extinguish the Holy Spirit of God. He means—Do not understand the Gospel in such a manner as to paralyse human romance or to crush human exaltation of spirit, or to damp down the desire for reformation, or to stifle the expression of human affection. Are not these movements of the spirits of men, even when they be altogether undisciplined, parables, witnesses, signposts by which we are led to conceive of the workings and operations of the Holy Spirit of God? And if our spirits are thus related to the Spirit of God, do they not become more than parables and signposts and tokens and witnesses? Do they not become, in this relativity, genuinely and essentially related to God, manifestations of His Glory?

Once again, my brothers in Christ, may I warn you that, as Christians and as men, you are moving along a path narrow and sharp as the edge of a razor, for on one side of you lies the blasphemy of human idolatry, and on the other side yawns the chasm of detachment and cynical aloofness? Between the two walked the Christ. He trod the road which led to death and He trod that road alone, but—and this is what I wish now to remind you of—He received and blessed and bade His followers never forget the action of the woman who impetuously and devotedly and beyond all reason, broke for His sake the alabaster cruse of very costly ointment and poured it over His head.

'Verily I say unto you, Wheresoever the Gospel shall be preached throughout the whole world, that also which this woman hath done shall be spoken of for a memorial of her.'

We may, perhaps, have been wise for Christ's sake, but have we ever been fools for Christ's sake? Or, for that matter, have we ever been fools for the sake of any other proper or improper cause whatever?

IV
THE HOMILIES

(1934–35)

I. INTRODUCTION

'Now it came to pass, that the people pressed upon him to hear the word of God.'   (St Luke v. 1.)

It is the responsibility of the Dean of Chapel to instruct you in this place concerning the doctrine of the Church of England. I have, therefore, now for many years taken as my subject some part of the Library which as laymen you have, or are supposed to have, in your hands—I mean, the Bible, the Book of Common Prayer, the Thirty-Nine Articles of Religion, and the Hymn Books. There is, however, another book to which reference is made both in the Articles and in the Book of Common Prayer, a book which you have not in your hands and with which you are presumably unfamiliar, but which seems to me nevertheless to be not unimportant at the present time. Though the book itself is not very easily accessible to you, yet the themes with which it deals are quite elemental, the language in which it is written is almost as classical as that of the English Bible and of the English Book of Common Prayer, and it comes from a period in English history when a large number of English men and women were possessed of a genuine sense for Christian Truth—I had almost said, of proper theological insight.

The XXXVth Article is entitled 'Of the Homilies', and runs as follows:

'The second Book of Homilies...doth contain a godly and wholesome Doctrine, and necessary for these times, as doth the former Book of Homilies, which were set forth in the time of *Edward* the Sixth;

and therefore we judge them to be read in Churches by the Ministers, diligently and distinctly, that they may be understanded of the people.'

The second rubric which follows the Creed in the Communion Service refers also to the Homilies:

'Then shall follow the Sermon, or one of the Homilies already set forth, or hereafter to be set forth, by authority.'

I propose therefore during these two winter terms to say something to you about these Homilies; not about their history, nor about the manner of their composition, not even about the nature of the authority with which they were set forth, but about their contents, about the themes with which they deal.

That these themes are not irrelevant will be at once clear from some of their titles.

The first Homily in the First Book is entitled 'A Fruitful Exhortation to the Reading of Holy Scripture.'

Homily VI. 'Of Christian Love and Charity.'
Homily VIII. 'Of the Declining from God.'
Homily XI. 'Against Whoredom and Adultery.'
Homily XII. 'Against Strife and Contention.'

In the Second Book, Homily II is entitled 'Against peril of Idolatry'.

Homily X. 'An Information of them which take offence at certain places of Holy Scripture.'
Homily XVIII. 'Of the state of Matrimony.'
Homily XXI. 'An Homily against Disobedience and wilful Rebellion.'

Let me first, however, say something to you about the problem in the Church which gives rise to authoritative Homilies.

The existence of Homilies raises, of course, the question of the speech of the Church; it raises also the question to whom the Church rightly speaks; and it raises finally the question of what ought to be said by the Church, if it is to be permitted to speak at all.

There have been times in the history of Christendom when the Church has relapsed into silence, or rather there have been times when the Church has been content to perform its Liturgy or repeat its Prayer Book. But it may be doubted to what extent a Church that has lost its voice is still a Christian Church, still bears witness to the Word of God, still worships the God Who spake and it was done, still in any way reflects the situation in which Jesus, surrounded by the crowds, spake the Word of God. The business of the world is after all carried on by words, and a Church which has nothing to say tends to become ineffective and in the end may do nothing at all.

It must, however, be admitted that more often the Church is very loquacious, indeed its ministers appear to do nothing but talk, and, when we ask what it is that they are saying, it seems that no more is being done than to echo the things which the men of the world were saying the day before yesterday, and so we get scraps of economic or psychological theory, bits of historical or medical information, fragments of moral and religious exhortations. And when we try to discover the coherence or relevance of what we have heard, the whole appears very undisciplined, very casual, and very unsatisfactory.

And yet, we ought not to be unsympathetic here with

our parish priests: for if once it be admitted that they must speak—well, they are men like you and me, and because they are men they have ideas in their heads, affections in their hearts, and deep convictions in their consciences; and if, when they mount the pulpits, it is to these things that they give utterance, we ought not to be surprised that it should be so; and if they are moved by this or that notion, stirred by this or that appeal, moved to this or that good work, carried off their feet by this or that aspect of religious piety—well, it is of this very human stuff that preachers are made, and it does at least shew that they are men of flesh and blood. But when all this is said, and when we have recovered our sympathy even with the clergy, still it is clear that something is going wrong as it has often gone wrong before with the speech of the Church. It is clear, too, that the Church cannot in the end exist if it merely echoes human opinions, human feelings, and human convictions and experiences, and is unable to relate all these things to the Truth of God and to see their final meaning in this relationship. In other words, if the pulpit is unable to declare the Word of God and to confront men and women by the meaning of their life and death, and is unable to see this meaning, not merely here and there, but in the quite ordinary experiences of human life, we must remember also that Christian Truth is not a thing which can be dumped down upon each generation like a cricket ball hurled at a number of batsmen, just with a certain deceptive variation in pace or break. Christian Truth lies in the stuff of which each generation is made, and there are times when it is not very easy to hear, not very easy to see, and not very easy to express.

No amount of ability and eloquence on the part of the preacher can compensate for the absence of a proper Gospel, for the Church stands or falls by whether it does or does not possess something which it is responsible to say, which makes sense not only of its own liturgy or worship and prayers, but of human life altogether.

This brings us to the third problem that underlies the English Homilies, namely, the question, To whom does the Church speak? We have almost become defeatists here, perhaps not unnaturally. We are apt to suppose that the Church speaks only to its own adherents, and the Church is consequently on the high road to become a group of pious people. But this is the end of the Church. It is the end of the Church if it regards what it has to say as relevant and audible only to a peculiar number of people. Not for one moment did those who composed the English Homilies suppose that what they had to say concerned only a minority of people. They wrote for the realm of England, and for this reason they wrote, not a compendium of speculative theology, however important that may be, but a series of Homilies to be read, to be preached, to the people of this country. They had not forgotten that the Lord spoke to the crowds, that the God whom they worshipped is the Creator of the universe visible and invisible, and that Jesus is the Lamb of God which taketh away the sin of the world. They had not forgotten that the Ten Commandments, though spoken originally to Israel, are for that very reason spoken to all men, and that they contain the ultimate imperative of God that men should worship Him and Him only, and that they should love their neighbours as they love themselves.

This sense for the responsibility of the Church to speak and to speak rightly and to speak to all, lay behind the making of the English Homilies. Nor was the making of authoritative Homilies a peculiar activity of the Church of England in the sixteenth century. The problem of what the Church is to say is a permanent ecclesiastical problem, which is not solved by simply permitting everybody to say what they like. St Augustine recommended the clergy to use the Homilies of St Chrysostom; the Homilies of the Venerable Bede were for a long time widely used by the English clergy; Aelfric, the Archbishop of York just before the Norman Conquest, issued a book of Homilies for the use of his clergy (of which we have no less than six copies in our Library); Charlemagne ordered Paul Warnefrid to make a collection of Homilies for use in the Gallican Church. When therefore the clergy of the Church of England were, during the sixteenth century, presented with two books of authoritative Homilies, no new demands were imposed upon them. They were warned that they were responsible to speak, and a serious attempt was made to ensure that they should speak properly.

My brothers in Christ, there can be no doubt that things have not so changed with us that the Church no longer has anything to say, but in the midst of so many voices the Word with which the Church has been entrusted is exceedingly difficult to hear, and even more difficult to voice. This being so, it can hardly be a waste of time to pick up once again the English Homilies in order to see whether perhaps it may not be possible with this assistance for the Church once again to recover its voice and something also of its ancient confidence.

II. OF DECLINING FROM GOD

'All the ends of the earth shall remember themselves and be turned unto the Lord; and all the kindreds of the nations shall worship before him.

For the kingdom is the Lord's.'

(Psalm xxii. 27–28.)

'Of our going from God, the Wise Man saith that pride was the first beginning: for by it man's heart was turned from God his Maker. *For pride* (saith he) *is the fountain of all sin: he that hath it shall be full of cursings, and at the end it shall overthrow him.*'

These are the opening words of the Homily entitled: 'A Sermon, how Dangerous a Thing it is to Fall from God.' This Homily is the eighth Homily in the First Book of the Church of England Homilies, and in the Table of contents it is entitled: 'Of the Declining from God.' The Wise Man to whom reference is made is, of course, the Wise Man in the tenth chapter of the Book of Ecclesiasticus.

I have decided to say something to you concerning what is contained in the two books of English Homilies because it can hardly be doubted that in spite of much talk about religion the Church has lost its voice, and because, this being a serious situation for us all, it may be possible to recover an understanding of the Truth entrusted to the Church and to restore confidence in the relevance of 'the faith once delivered to the saints', if we pay attention to what is said in the famous, but seldom read, Homilies of the Church of England, even though these Homilies were composed and handed over to the clergy and people of England in the sixteenth century. In this College, moreover, they ought not to be neglected, since Archbishop Parker, to whom we are indebted for more than the gift of plate and manuscripts, himself composed one of the Homilies—the Homily for the Days of Rogation Week, in which we are exhorted to 'raise up some motion of thanksgiving to the goodness of Almighty God'—and since it was the Archbishop who presented the Second Book of Homilies to Queen Elizabeth, the unique copy which he had procured to be handsomely bound for presentation to Her Majesty being now in the British Museum.

Having decided that we ought for reasons both private and public to know something about these Homilies, it has not been easy for me to make up my mind with which of the thirty-three Homilies to begin. There was something, in view of the visit of the King and Queen to Cambridge, to be said for starting with the Homily 'Against Disobedience and Wilful Rebellion'; something, in view of the themes of much recent literature, for starting with the Homily 'Against Whoredom and Adultery', or with the Homily 'Of the State of Matrimony'; more, perhaps, to be said for starting where the Homilies themselves start, with the 'Fruitful Exhortation to the Reading and Knowledge of Holy Scripture' and with the surely magnificent first sentence of the first Homily:

'Unto a Christian man there can be nothing either more necessary or more profitable than the knowledge of holy Scripture....'

And yet we have to recognise that for a large number of Englishmen this appeal to Scripture is no longer final, the authority of the Bible has become itself a problem, and in many even religious quarters not even a problem, only a relic of antiquity which is widely supposed to be no longer relevant. There is for us a previous question, the question of the declining or falling from God altogether. It is this terrible situation which is dealt with in the eighth Homily of the First Book. And it is, I think, there that we are bound to start, even though we shall find that in handling this as in handling other themes the authors of the English Homilies can never escape from the language of the Bible, can never speak as though it did not exist, can never avoid illustrating what they have to say from Biblical scenes however rough these scenes may be. For, to the authors of the Homilies, the ultimate truths about human life were not new truths requiring new formulation. The truth had already been seen, apprehended, and uttered: it had been seen, apprehended, and uttered by prophets and apostles. All that the authors of the Homilies felt to be new in this country was that what apostles and prophets had said was now generally accessible to English people in the recently printed English Bible. The authors of the Homilies did not, however, for one moment suppose that to have translated and published the English Bible was in itself sufficient. The themes of the Bible required to be known and apprehended, and it was still necessary to make their relevance to English life plain and unmistakable. It was for this reason that the Homilies were ordered to be read in the churches, for this reason also that the titles were so carefully chosen, in order that the relevance

of the Bible to the ordinary, straightforward and fundamental things of all human life should be at once recognisable. The visible world, men, marriage, babies and
the manner in which they come into the world, war,
famine, prosperity, success, bread, death, the relation
of a man to his neighbour, these are the themes of the
Homilies, just as they are the themes of the Bible: and,
after all, these are not irrelevant things; they cannot be
dismissed as uncomfortable relics of antiquity.

Behind all these seemingly fragmentary, episodic
occurrences, however, lies the relation of the world to
its Maker, the relation of men to God. In this relationship consists the meaning of the world of men and of
things. This is the primary and ultimate theme of the
Homilies as it is of the Bible, and it is this theme which
saves human life from being merely fragmentary,
episodic, and finally chaotic.

It is this first and last truth, this meaning of history,
which compels the theologian to deal seriously with the
straightforward visible world, and which demands of
the preacher and of the parish priest that they should
care for what is taking place before their eyes, because
history is the place where the revelation of God is made
known. It is this first and last truth which at times
compels the historian also to long for theology to appear
as a proper and relevant subject, and which also at times
causes the man of the world to turn towards the Church
hoping that there his poverty, his unexpected failures
may be explained.

But in spite of this criss-cross movement of the men of
the world towards God and of the men of God towards
the world, we have to own that for the most part there

is no such movement. For the most part we are blind to this essential relation between God and the world, between God and ourselves. In the eighth Homily this blindness of ours is taken seriously, it is named a dangerous thing, so dangerous that in the second part of the Homily the possibility, nay the certainty, is recognised that not only can we and do we turn from God, but He also turns from us and leaves us alone in our liberty.

Listen to this remarkable passage on the subject of liberty, a passage which ought not to remain unknown, so surprisingly appropriate is it.

The Homily has been speaking about the visible active warnings of God—of famine, battle, dearth and death. It then proceeds:

'Finally, if these do not serve, God will let us lie waste; he will give us over; he will turn away from us; he will dig and delve no more about us; he will let us alone, and suffer us to bring forth even such fruit as we will, to bring forth brambles, briars, and thorns, all naughtiness, all vice, and that so abundantly that they shall clean overgrow us, choke, strangle and utterly destroy us. But they that in this world live not after God, but after their own carnal liberty, perceive not this great wrath of God towards them, that he will dig nor delve any more about them, that he doth let them alone even to themselves: but they take this for a great benefit of God, to have all at their own liberty: and so they live, as carnal liberty were the true liberty of the Gospel. But God forbid, good people, that ever we should desire such liberty.'

The author of the Homily did at any rate recognise that when we have spoken the word 'liberty', we have not of necessity spoken the final word: it may indeed be no more than the sign, not merely that we have turned away from God, but that He also has turned away His face from us. If all this seems strange to us, are we quite certain that what is being said is untrue?

The English Homilies are grave and serious things. Nowhere are they trivial, nowhere are they frivolous or cheap or superficial, nowhere do they pretend that human life is not a grave matter fraught here and now with big issues. But this gravity is not due to any detachment from life as it is: it is not, I think, due to any innate profundity of soul on the part of the men who wrote them. The Homilies were not written by men of strong convictions; they do not give the impression of being clever; nor do they contain personal opinions or speculations; nor were they written on the background of careful metaphysical training. The Homilies are serious for one reason and for one reason only: they were written by men who had taken God seriously as the Creator of the world. It followed of necessity that they could not think of religion as of some kind of piety added to human life. They could not think (say) of the Church of England as existing in its own right in some kind of independent position: entrusted with a responsibility towards the people of England, it must speak or die, and it must speak only about God, for it had no other right to exist. For they knew that it was really possible for the people of England to decline from God, that it was possible for them to turn from God by falling into idolatry, by lack of faith, by neglecting their neighbours, by not hearing God's word, and by the pleasure they took in the vanity of worldly things.

It is with these things that the eighth Homily in the First Book deals, and with the reverse side of the picture, with the real possibility that when we have turned from God, He may turn from us.

III. ARMISTICE DAY

'According to the law I may almost say, All things are cleansed with blood, and apart from shedding of blood there is no remission of sin....So Christ was once offered to bear the sins of many.'

(Hebrews ix. 22, 28.)

When Armistice Day falls, as it does this year (1934), upon a Sunday, it is clear, even if we had not recognised it before, that the State and the Church are using similar, if not identical, language to express a common grief and distress, and to express also a common hope. This common language is not due to some borrowing by the State of the language of the Church. The Church is the borrower, when, in order to express its theme, it is compelled to use language rooted in the experience of War. In human history great issues have been fought out by war, and war means death: it means great misery and distress: but war means also the victory of one side or the other; and victory means peace—at least for a period of time. Peace, Victory, Death: Death, Victory, Peace: these are words fashioned in the rough world of human affairs, and to them the Church has turned when it comes to express its own insight into Truth. When, therefore, the Christian proclaims Christus Victor, it suggests and is meant to suggest that the experience of war is relevant, if not indeed essential, for the understanding of the Gospel with which the Church has been entrusted. The Victory of Christ is, moreover, no easy, obvious victory. 'I have overcome the world' is a claim spoken in the Fourth Gospel over a scene of the outpouring of blood, spoken over the death of Jesus; and, moreover, these words were spoken also over the Church at the beginning of the second century, when after the death of the Christ, and in spite of His victory, there was no obvious, visible peace for His followers. It was still required of them that they should carry on the cause for which He died, still required of them that they should be ready to take up their cross and follow Him.

This overlapping of Church and State is a significant thing; this dependence of the Church upon the ordinary experiences of human life, and especially upon those experiences, such as war and peace, which are most elemental, is surely a very significant thing indeed. Significant, because it means that, as Christians, we must be prepared to see things as they are, and not merely as we should like them to be. The realism of the Church, when it is true to itself, is the most remarkable thing about it. The Church does dare to speak, as the second Homily does, of 'the Misery of all Mankind'; it refuses to permit us to be complacent. The Church does dare to speak, as the thirteenth Homily of the Second Book does, 'concerning the Death and Passion of our Saviour Christ'. It does not speak only of beauty and of truth and of goodness, but also of what is ugly and untrue; in fact, it speaks much of sin and of iniquity and of the punishment of sin.

And so, if the Church speaks, as it must do, of the remission of sins, it can do so only in the context of the death of Christ, as the author of the Epistle to the Hebrews has seen so clearly, since he has seen the bitter universal truth that all things, or almost all things, are cleansed by blood.

This is all no doubt very rough language, and it is to many a very shocking world, this world of Christian thought and experience. But we ought to be under no illusions here. It is not the idealism of the Church, but its realism, which is so disturbing and uncomfortable. And let us remember that the idealism of the Church rests upon its realism: they are not two separable things, one of which can be accepted and the other rejected: they cohere together. And when we speak of the realism of the Church, we do not mean merely that it takes the death of Christ seriously, but also that it takes equally seriously the rough things of human life altogether, and plunges its sons and daughters into that roughness. The Church moves from the life of the Commonwealth or State to its own Gospel. Listen to the movement of the opening paragraph of the Church's Homily for Good Friday:

'If a mortal man's deed done to the behoof of the commonwealth be had in remembrance of us, with thanks for the benefit and profit which we receive thereby, how much more readily should we have in memory this excellent act and benefit of Christ's death; whereby he hath purchased for us the undoubted pardon and forgiveness of our sins; whereby he made at one the Father of heaven with us, in such wise that he taketh us now for his loving children, and for the true *inheritors with Christ*, his natural Son, of the Kingdom of heaven!'

Thus Christians are bidden to pass from a national commemoration to the commemoration of the death of Christ, from the commemoration of the benefits which we have received of the one to the benefit which we receive of the other, since there is a correspondence between them.

What, therefore, do we in fact commemorate to-day as Englishmen? First, this country was called upon to face a great issue, an issue which presented itself, not in terms of economic development or of private quarrelling or jealousy, but in terms of right and wrong. This country found itself confronted by what it was unable to describe otherwise than as an evil thing. Secondly, the issue was so serious, so deep-seated, that conference, discussion, good-will, persuasion, and all the other more normal methods of settling mere disagreements had been found to be unavailing. This country was, therefore, compelled to take up the only course left to it: it was compelled to fight. Thirdly, having decided to fight, the Commonwealth has had to learn what war means. The meaning of war needs no description to-day. We do not need to be reminded that war means death, that it means the real outpouring of a country's blood, that it means great poverty, distress and misery. Then, fourthly —and we must not forget this—we do commemorate a victory. The enemy was beaten in the end. How nearly this was not so, you all know. But this country was preserved from defeat, and for this, if we be not altogether inhuman, we are bound to be grateful, grateful to those who were our protection. Finally, we are also bound to speak the word 'peace'. At last, on the other side of victory came peace—the cessation of war.

All this, and much more, we commemorate to-day. We commemorate a bit of genuine history. These things really took place. They are rough, they are horrible, but they did happen. The words right, wrong, battle, war, sacrifice, victory, defeat, peace, are words which belong to the world in which we live, words which have been formulated out of the stuff of which human life is made.

Now, are we to regard all this as trivial and without meaning? Are we to say it was all a ghastly mistake? Are we to say that there was no issue and that human life was merely thrown away? This is surely to play with the real world, and if we play with history here, shall we not be driven to play with it all along the line, until we become purely frivolous?

No doubt, this bit of history is a very human affair. No doubt, the words we use to describe it are big words which, we know only too well, do not altogether fit. We speak of 'a great issue', but when we try to define what it was precisely, we find ourselves involved in serious difficulties. We speak of 'right' and 'wrong', of 'good' and 'evil', and we must so speak; but when we describe ourselves as right and good, we know that the description does not fit us, and we grow so uncomfortable that we are shy of using ethical language at all, and fall back into talking about economic pressure. We speak of 'victory' and of 'peace', and yet the words tremble on our lips, for what is our victory, and what is the peace which we have achieved? So acutely do many of our contemporaries feel these words to be irrelevant that they speak of the defeat of those who were victorious and of the turmoil of the peace. These insistent question marks must not, however, be permitted to deprive us of the language of war. For it is this language that sets us, if we do not shirk it, in the presence of the ultimate moral issues of right and wrong, of an ultimate Cause which must be completely and victoriously won, which requires an ultimate sacrifice, and which, being won, does veritably bring peace to the world.

And so the commemoration of Armistice Day requires a Gospel to make sense of it, for otherwise the language of war and peace must remain almost altogether halting and uncertain. With this Gospel the Church of Christ has been entrusted. But it is no easy Gospel, for though it speaks of the peace of God which passeth all understanding, it cannot speak of peace save in the context of war, in the context of the death of Christ, and of that death as a sacrifice. Nor can it speak of peace save in the context of ultimate victory over evil. The Christian word 'peace' is not merely the opposite of war, for even if we could abolish war we should not have peace. Peace is the opposite of Sin. Peace is the final union of God and man. Peace is the destruction of evil altogether. Peace is that for which we hope and in which we believe, through Jesus Christ our Lord.

IV. OF THE RIGHT USE OF THE CHURCH OR TEMPLE OF GOD

'They found him in the Temple.'

(St Luke ii. 46.)

Joseph and Mary were first astonished, then put out. They expected their son either to be playing with His friends or not to have strayed beyond the immediate ken of His parents. They found Him in the Temple, and He is surprised at this ignorance, for the Temple in Jerusalem was His Father's House. They found Him in the midst of the doctors, and He is surprised that they should think this strange company for a boy.

The comment on this passage in the relevant Homily of the Church of England runs as follows:

'If we lack Jesus Christ, that is to say, the Saviour of our souls and bodies, we shall not find him in the market place, or in the guild hall, much less in the alehouse or tavern amongst good fellows (as they call them), so soon as we shall find him in the temple, the Lord's house, amongst the teachers and preachers of his word. . . .'

And we may note in passing, first, that the Homily does not say that Jesus Christ cannot be found in the market-place, or in the place where human affairs are locally ordered, nor that He cannot be found among good fellows in a tavern. What it says is, that He can be more clearly discovered within the walls of the House of God. Secondly, we may also take particular notice of the confidence of the author of the Homily that, in spite of grave religious controversy and disturbance, and in spite of very great clerical omission and disorder, the Word of God was in fact spoken in the churches of this country in the middle of the sixteenth century, and spoken moreover more clearly than elsewhere. The Homily means, of course, that in the churches up and down the country, in spite of much inadequacy on the part of the clergy, the Bible is publicly read and the Sacraments are administered. It means also—for the Homilies of the Church of England are never anti-clerical, they do not harp upon clerical impotence, they do not undermine the work of the parish clergy in this country—that even the weakest sermon, the weakest preacher, does speak about God and not merely about men, does speak about Jesus Christ, and not merely about himself.

The Homilies of the Church of England—which I have ventured to take as providing the basis of this year's sermons in this place—were concerned to recover among the laity of this country an understanding of what it means to be a Christian layman, of his duties and responsibilities, and of the extreme dignity of his position; dignity, I mean, in the sense that the Homilies assume that grave issues are at stake in all this, grave issues for the health and stability of the Commonwealth of England. The Church in this country is not a trivial thing, nor is it an institution existing apart from the life of the country as a whole. It has a mission to fulfil, a mission quite impossible if the Church be thought of merely as a body of clerics or as a group of pietists.

When the authors of the Homilies come to define what a Christian is, they lay down first the importance of a knowledge of Holy Scripture—that, as we have seen, is the subject of the first Homily in the First Book—and then they call attention to the importance of a right use of the churches, I mean the buildings, scattered up and down the country. This forms the subject of the first Homily in the Second Book, of the Homily entitled, 'Of the Right Use of the Church or Temple of God, and of the Reverence due unto the same', which was written, or seems to have been written, by Bishop Jewel.

The Homily opens with the following words:

'Where[as] there appeareth at these days great slackness and negligence of a great sort of people in resorting to the church, there to serve God their heavenly Father according to their most bounden duty...; and thereby may just fear arise of the wrath of God...for our grievous offence in this behalf...: therefore I pray you give good audience....'

(The ego here is not merely the 'I' of the author of the Homily, but of the parish clergyman who was ordered to read these Homilies to the people.)

It is perhaps worth while pausing here for a moment to point out that lack of knowledge and understanding of Scriptures and neglect of public worship were stated to be the two most subtly disintegrating forces at work in this country in the middle of the sixteenth century. We must therefore, I think, beware of supposing that, when we are confronted by a similar disintegration, we are faced by a new problem occasioned by the emergence of some new kind of civilisation which makes the Scriptures and the Church altogether out of date, and which means that we, who are responsible for upholding the

Christian religion, belong to an age that is gone, and that at best the Church is no more than a valuable brake applied to the movement of progress which, when it has found its new equilibrium, will require no such brake; so that, in the end, the Church and the Scriptures will remain mere relics of an outworn civilisation. This seems, however, to be a wholly false analysis. The problem with which we are confronted is essentially the same problem which the Church has always had to face when new forces arise in a civilisation which has appeared more stable than it really is. However this may be, the problem of the meaning of Scripture and the problem of the meaning of the Church were urgent questions in the sixteenth century, and it can hardly be doubted that they are so now. Then, as now, they were questions which could not be left to the clergy: they were and are important questions for the laymen also. They concern us all.

When we have said this, certain things must be borne in mind, things which are clearly laid down in the Homily of the Right Use of the Church or Temple of God.

When the layman of the Church of England recognises and accepts the duty of attendance at public worship in Church, he does not thereby deny—I am quoting the Homily—'the eternal and incomprehensible Majesty of God, the *Lord of heaven and earth*, whose *seat is heaven and the earth his footstool*'. Nor does he do something that undermines the truth evidently declared by the prophet Isaiah, by St Stephen, and by St Paul, that the incomprehensible Majesty of God 'cannot be enclosed *in temples* or houses *made with* man's *hand*'. The

God whom we worship in His House or Temple is the invisible Creator and Sustainer of all visible things.

To quote again the Homily:

> 'The material church or temple is a place appointed, as well by the usage and continual examples expressed in the Old Testament as in the New, for the people of God to resort together unto, there to hear God's holy word, to call upon his holy Name, to give him thanks for his innumerable and unspeakable benefits bestowed upon us, and duly and truly to celebrate his holy Sacraments.'

The Church or Temple of God in our midst is, then, undoubtedly the place where the incomprehensible Majesty of God is set forth to us, and set forth to us most clearly in the visible life and death of our Saviour Jesus Christ.

Nor does the act of public worship deny that the Temples of God in which He chiefly and most especially delighteth to dwell and continue in, are the bodies and minds of true Christians, as the Homily, echoing St Paul, quite clearly states. But which of us dare to say of ourselves that we do in fact glorify God in our bodies or in our minds or in our souls? That we desire to do so, which is the only proper act of witness of which we are most of us capable, requires some public act on our part, and for this act of witness our churches exist.

Lastly—and this is the main point of the Homily—the sanctuary, or house, or temple, or tabernacle, or synagogue, is a major theme of the Scriptures. These words occur, as the Homily says, in almost infinite places of the Scripture. It is a genuine and sometimes wilful misreading of Scripture to suppose that either the Jews or the primitive Christians assembled together for the most part in the open air, on the green grass, or in the street, and not in some place in some way set apart for the worship of God. Paul and Barnabas preached the Word of God on the Sabbath day in the synagogue or church, and only when they were thrust out thence did they have to find some other place. This does not, of course, mean that the Word of God could only be spoken in a church or temple or synagogue, but it does mean that it was spoken there, and that people did congregate there expecting to hear the Word of God spoken by prophets and priests, and that these expectations were fulfilled, if not by the presence of a prophet in their midst, at least by the reading of the Scriptures, by the singing of the Psalter, and, in the Temple at Jerusalem, by the token and sign of Jewish sacrifice.

Nor ought we, for one moment, to suppose that our Lord spoke only in the open air. Jesus in the synagogues on the Sabbath is a continuous theme in the Gospels. Does not Luke indeed open his account of our Lord's ministry in Galilee with the narrative of the famous scene in the synagogue at Nazareth? And when we come to the picture of the Lord in Jerusalem, the Temple is the chief scene of His Ministry there, and it is so not primarily because the crowds were there, but because, as He says, it is His Father's House. When we come to the Fourth Gospel the great discourses to the crowds are most of them spoken in the Temple.

These things we must not forget when we have to consider our Christian duties, and when we have to face a situation not unlike that in the middle of the sixteenth century when the Church of England found a large defection of those who were meant to compose its laity.

The question of the duty of public worship is one which requires very plain speaking to-day, plainer speaking than I find myself capable of. The case is, however, overwhelming, and it must not be permitted to go by default.

V. OF GOOD ORDER AND OBEDIENCE

'Hear therefore, ye kings, and understand;
Learn, ye judges of the ends of the earth;
Give ear, ye that have dominion over much people,
. . . .
that your dominion was given you from the Lord
and your sovereignty from the Most High
who shall search out your works, and make inquisition
    of your counsels.'

           (Wisdom of Solomon vi. 1–3.)

There was, then, a time in this country when the Queen (Elizabeth), acting on the advice of her 'most honourable counsellors', commanded all 'Parsons, Vicars, Curates, and all other having spiritual cure' to read and declare plainly and distinctly to their parishioners, 'every Sunday and Holy Day in the year', one of the Homilies which had been set forth by her brother Edward the Sixth. For this purpose the Queen ordered the Book of Homilies to be printed anew, and gave particular instruction that they were to be read at the ministering of Holy Communion or, if there were no

Communion ministered on that particular Sunday or Holy Day, a Homily was to be read nevertheless after the Gospel and Creed.

There were three chief reasons for the Queen's action, and they were set out in the preface to the 1562 edition of the Homilies. She and her principal advisers were aware that 'corrupt, vicious, and ungodly living' among many of her subjects was causing considerable difficulty to her government; secondly, they found that the Church upon which rested the chief responsibility for expelling and driving away this corruption of morals, was crippled because it was itself not free from 'erroneous and poisoned doctrines'; and thirdly, it was discovered that many of the appointed ministers were not in possession of the gift of preaching sufficiently to instruct the people.

Some honest remedy was urgently required to meet this situation, and the republication of the Homilies and the enforcement of their reading was the remedy proposed and acted upon.

Last term I ventured to bring to your notice the subject-matter of some of these forgotten Homilies. There is, however, included in them much more that is, I think, worthy of your consideration as Christians; and therefore I must invite your attention to some more themes of the Christian religion, and ask you to be patient with the form in which these themes were presented to this country at what was surely a classical period in its history: and by 'classical' I mean a period when quite elemental problems of human life were so naked that no one in his senses could fail to see them, and a period also in which important things were said to Englishmen about these problems and said to them in such a manner that they were compelled in their necessity and tribulation to listen to them: classical also because in this situation it was to the Church that those responsible for the proper government of the country found they were bound to look, for, so long as the pulpit remained either silent or irresponsible, the situation in the country seemed wellnigh hopeless. In short, the period was classical because things that are always present in human life lay so near to the surface.

It is not surprising therefore to find the Homilies dealing quite frankly with whoredom and adultery, with contention and brawling, with gluttony and drunkenness, with good order and obedience, and then jumping, not, however, irrelevantly, to speak of the Death of Christ, of Prayer, and of the Sacraments of the Church.

In the Homilies the elemental facts of quite normal human life are interlocked with the deepest truths of the Christian religion in such a manner that it is impossible to hold them apart. This is nowhere so clear as it is when the Homilies come to deal with order and disorder, with obedience and with rebellion. The Homilies under the title of 'An Exhortation concerning Good Order and Obedience to Rulers and Magistrates'—and there are no less than nine of them in the two Books—are perhaps the most difficult for us to understand and appreciate. It is easy to say that they are Erastian (whatever that word may be supposed to mean), or that they are harping on one side of a very difficult problem, or that they have not formulated properly the problem of the nature of authority in Church and State, that they rest upon an uncritical attitude to the Bible, and so on and so forth. All this seems to me to be largely wide of the mark. The most striking fact about these Homilies is that the Queen and her advisers, though they were faced by grave disorders in the country and by the imminent possibility of rebellion, do not seem for one moment to have thought of asking the Church to speak about discipline. What they required of the Church was that it should not be afraid to speak about its own proper themes, about Order and about Obedience, about the Order of God and about Obedience to Him, and that it should speak about these things, not in a vacuum in which only God and the people existed, but in the midst of the real world in which distinctions, proper distinctions, existed, and in which harmony and order also existed because of a strict relationship and coherence between these distinctions.

If the Queen demanded obedience to herself and to her magistrates, she did not ask the Church to speak merely of this, but to speak of it in the context of obedience to God on which the whole order of the Universe depends. Now, the Queen did not merely *ask* this of the Church, she *demanded* it, not because she wished to tyrannise over her people, but in order to make tyranny impossible: for government must either tyrannise or abdicate if those who exercise authority are not themselves under authority; and it must also tyrannise or abdicate if it be widely supposed that liberty and freedom are things which exist by and in themselves and are not the fruits of obedience, and of that obedience which cannot, without disaster, come to rest anywhere short of obedience to God.

It is to the opening sentences of the Homilies concerning Good Order and Obedience to Rulers and Magistrates that I would now therefore direct your attention. These opening sentences are not merely formal: they express the heart of the whole matter, and all that follows depends upon them. And we must not forget, when we hear them, that these opening sentences were not invented to meet a particular situation in England during the sixteenth century, nor were they just formulating a sort of ecclesiastical worldly wisdom: they express, and express quite simply, the truth apart from which not only is the Church itself nonsense, but the Evangelical record of the death of Jesus, that is to say, of His submission to Pilate, is also nonsense.

And now for the opening sentences of the Homilies. They are all of them amplifications of the first words of the Collect for St Michael and All Angels' Day, with which you are probably familiar. The Collect begins: 'O everlasting God, who hast ordained and constituted the services of Angels and men in a wonderful Order.' Here is the juxtaposition of God and Order. Think theologically and you are bound to speak of Order and not of chaos. Address God in prayer and you are bound to recognise the orderly character of the world in which you live, since it is the creation of Him to whom the Church addresses its prayers and for whose glory the Church exists.

Listen now to the opening words of the first of the Homilies concerning Order:

'Almighty God hath created and appointed all things, in heaven, earth, and waters, in a most ex-cellent and perfect order. In heaven he hath appointed distinct and several orders and states of archangels and angels. In earth he hath assigned and appointed kings and princes, with other governors under them, all in good and necessary order.... The earth, trees, seeds, plants, herbs, corn, grass, and all manner of beasts, keep themselves in their order. All the parts of the whole year, as winter, summer, months, nights, and days, continue in their order. All kinds of fishes in the sea, rivers and waters, with all fountains and springs, yea, the seas themselves, keep their comely course and order. And man himself also hath all his parts within and without, as soul, heart, mind, memory, understanding, reason, speech, with all and singular corporal members of his body, in a profitable, necessary, and pleasant order. Every degree of people in their vocation, calling, and office, hath appointed to them their duty and order. Some are in high degree, some in low; some kings and princes, some inferiors and subjects; priests and laymen, masters and servants, fathers and children, husbands and wives, rich and poor; and every one have need of other. So that in all things is to be lauded and praised the goodly order of God: without the which no house, no city, no commonwealth can continue and endure; for, where there is no right order, there reigneth all abuse, carnal liberty, enormity, sin, and Babylonical confusion. Take away kings, princes, rulers, magistrates, judges, and such estates of God's order, no man shall ride or go by the highway unrobbed; no man shall sleep in his own house or bed unkilled; no man shall keep his wife, children and possessions in quietness; all things shall be common; and there must needs follow all mischief and utter destruction both of souls, bodies, goods, and commonwealths. But blessed be God that we in this realm of England feel not the horrible calamities, miseries, and wretchedness, which all they undoubtedly feel and suffer that lack this godly order.'

The meaning of all this is clear enough. Order is a proper Christian word and obedience is a proper Christian duty, not because order is a thing imposed by us, rightly or wrongly, upon an otherwise chaotic material, but because order lies at the heart and structure of human life. This order is, however, not a thing in itself which may be taken up, examined, and accepted or cast aside. It is the Order of God, the witness of the creation to its Creator. Remove all thought of the Order of God, cease to worship Him and pray to Him, abandon the honour and praise that is due to Him, and government soon either shews itself harsh and tyrannical, or loses its confidence in its responsibility of government; and this alternative of tyranny or of abdication extends down till it affects the order of a family and of all other smaller corporations and societies within the state.

It is in the Church that we learn these things, and for this reason the Church is not a private assembly of pietists but a necessity for the commonwealth. It may be that we shall have to learn these things over again, and it may be that the successors of Elizabeth will be compelled to lay their hands upon the Church and require of it that it shall speak of its proper theme, that it shall speak of God, lest both rulers and ruled alike perish for lack of knowledge in the midst of information.

VI. OF WHOREDOM AND UNCLEANNESS

'There shall be no whore among the daughters of Israel, nor whoremonger among the sons of Israel.'
(Deuteronomy xxiii. 17.)

I wish to say something to you this evening about the subject-matter of the eleventh Homily of the First Book, which is entitled 'A Sermon against Whoredom and Uncleanness, in three Parts', and something also about the long Homily in the Second Book which treats 'of the State of Matrimony'.

Last Sunday we saw how Queen Elizabeth laid hold of the Church and required of it that it should speak of its proper theme and that it should dare to speak with authority; how she required in particular that it should speak of the Order that is made known in the structure of the created universe, and that it should lay upon Christians the consequent duty of obedience.

There was, however, another evil which pressed hardly upon the Queen and her most honourable counsellors, and with which they were unable to deal should the Church continue to remain silent. In the Preface to the 1562 edition of the First Book of the Homilies, the Queen refers to 'corrupt, vicious, and ungodly living' as one of the chief reasons why she had decided that it was urgently necessary for the Church to speak to her people. The Church must speak, in order that corrupt and vicious living might be expelled and driven away by the setting forth of the principal points of the Christian religion and by the declaring of the

Word of God 'which is the principal guide and leader unto all godliness and virtue'. So the Queen wrote, and that she was thinking primarily of the widespread 'breaking of wedlock' which was springing up in serious form in the country is clear from the manner in which whoredom is spoken of in the Homilies themselves: and by whoredom was meant not merely prostitution, but, as whoredom is defined in the first Part of the Homily, 'all unlawful use of those parts which be ordained for generation'.

Listen to the opening paragraph of the first Part.

'Although there want not, good Christian people, great swarms of vices worthy to be rebuked, unto such decay is true godliness and virtuous living now come, yet above other vices the outrageous seas of adultery (or breaking of wedlock), whoredom, fornication, and uncleanness have not only burst in, but also over-flowed almost the whole world, unto the great dis-honour of God, the exceeding infamy of the name of Christ, the notable decay of true religion, and the utter destruction of the public wealth; and that so abundantly that, through the customable use thereof, this vice is grown into such an height, that in a manner among many it is accounted no sin at all, but rather a pastime, a dalliance, and but a touch of youth; not rebuked, but winked at; not punished, but laughed at.'

More serious even than the fact of adultery is stated to be the complacency of the adulterer. A paragraph in the second Part begins: 'For hath not the adulterer a pride in his whoredom? As the Wise Man saith: *They are glad*

*when they have done evil, and rejoice in things that are stark
naught.*' Hence the time has come when all degrees
must 'be monished, whether they be married or unmarried, to love chastity and cleanness of life. For the
married are bound by the law of God so purely to love
one another, that neither of them seek any strange love.
The man must only cleave to his wife, and the wife
again only to her husband. They must so delight in one
another's company, that none of them covet any other.
And, as they are bound thus to live together in all
godliness and honesty, so likewise it is their duty
virtuously to bring up their children, and to provide
that they fall not into Satan's snare nor into any uncleanness, but that they come pure and honest unto
holy wedlock when time requireth.'

It is clear, then, that the general situation was serious,
so serious that the primary problem of moral behaviour
could not be treated as a topic for debate, nor as an
opportunity for raising the difficulties occasioned by
hard cases, nor could it be set out adequately by means
of a series of extracts from some manual of Christian or
general Ethics. The Homily against Whoredom reads
as though the Church knows that it has its back against
the wall, that it can give no quarter and must display
no weakness here. A point has been reached where the
Church is fighting for the truth which has been entrusted
to it, and where it has been made aware, through the
insistence of the Queen, that it has to fight not merely
for itself, but for the right-mindedness of the people of
this country. The Church of England was thus thrust
back on its foundations, and it knew that it must speak
frankly or be dispossessed; that it must speak frankly at

least to those to whom it had the right to speak. Strange, and yet, when you come to think of it, not strange, that both Church and State should be forced back on their foundations by the fact of marriage and its disruption. One of the impressive things about this Homily is the complete absence of sentimentality. There is no going to sleep on phrases like the 'sanctity of marriage' or the 'beauty of the home'; no trace of any superstition about the 'marriage ceremony'. Marriage is a serious, dangerous and difficult occupation, which requires great care on both sides at the beginning, in the middle, and at the end, lest the forces of evil disrupt it; and they are real forces of evil.

Now, the Homily asserts three things:

First, Whoredom is a real evil.

Secondly, Wedlock is a condition of life ordained by God.

Thirdly, Matrimony is a state which requires strict attention on the part of both the contracting parties.

Throughout the Homily these are the things upon which emphasis is laid. But the Homilies are never secular. The Church addresses Christians as Christians and sees the whole antithesis of Whoredom and Matrimony in the perspective of Christian faith and practice. There is in the Homilies no trace at all of a worldly-wise treatment of these questions. They presume that Christians accept the authority of prophets and apostles, that they accept Jesus as One Who is able to issue commands which must be obeyed, and they presume, in addition, that a Christian may not unreasonably be expected to say his prayers. But there is no superstition in the way these aspects of Christian piety are described or applied. Christian belief and practice are treated as strictly relevant to so fundamental a situation as that presented by the fact or possibility of marriage. They are, therefore, relevant both to those who are married and to those who will in all probability have to undertake the responsibility at some future time. Christian belief is, therefore, important for both the married and the unmarried. And teaching about whoredom and matrimony must be public and not infrequent.

Nor in all this teaching about whoredom and marriage was the proper celibate person left without guidance. Celibacy is stated to be a vocation, but it is a vocation which, like marriage itself, requires care. At the end of the third part of the Homily occurs the following passage:

> 'All such as feel in themselves a sufficiency and ability, through the working of God's spirit, to lead a sole and continent life, let them praise God for his gift, and seek all means possible to maintain the same; as by reading of holy Scriptures, by godly meditations, by continual prayers, and such other virtuous exercises.'

The bachelor is thus compelled to recognise that he may become a dangerous person.

But the majority are not called to celibacy, and therefore, after bringing all Christians under the clear imperative of God that whoredom is an evil thing which must be shunned; and after making it quite plain that there is really no escape from the commandment of Christ:

> 'How can we be free from this commandment, where so great charge is laid upon us? May a servant do what he will in any thing, having a commandment

of his master to the contrary? Is not Christ our
Master? are not we his servants? How then may we
neglect our Master's will and pleasure, and follow our
own will and phantasy? *Ye are my friends*, saith Christ,
if you keep those things that I command you';

and after laying all this down with quite overwhelming
appeal to Scripture, the Homilies settle steadily down
to rid people's minds of any relics of a puritanical
attitude to marriage, as though it were not a state
instituted by God, a state in which a good conscience
may be preserved by both parties, a kind of life by means
of which the Church of God, and His Kingdom, may
be enlarged. Marriage must therefore be acknowledged
by Christians to be a benefit of God, His singular gift.

And then comes, what is also reinforced by the appeal
to Scripture, the instruction to the man and the woman,
the Homily of the State of Matrimony, from which I
cannot resist a few quotations.

The author of the Homily is now addressing directly
the married people.

'I would not have you careless, without watching.
For the devil will assay...to break this godly knot
once begun betwixt you, or else at the least he will
labour to encumber it with divers griefs and dis-
pleasures...Wherefore married persons must apply
their minds in most earnest wise to concord, and must
crave continually of God the help of his Holy Spirit...
to rule their hearts and to knit their minds together....
This necessity of prayer must be oft in the practice
and using of married persons, that ofttime the one
should pray for the other....'

Then the husband is directed to remember not only that the wife is the more frail party, but that he should not forget that the wife hath relinquished the liberty of her own rule, that she has consented not only to the pain of travailing, but also to the responsibility of the bringing up of young children. Gentleness and humanity are, therefore, required of the husband: but the wife must not abuse the gentleness of her Christian husband.

I have called your attention to these things, for it does not seem to be irrelevant that you should sometimes have them in your minds, lest you be not warned and prepared.

VII. OF STRIFE AND CONTENTION

'If it be possible, as much as in you lieth, live peaceably with all men.'   (Romans xii. 18.)

These be words of St Paul, and they are indeed, as the Homily says, 'full of stomach'.

I wish to speak to you this evening about Anger. The relevant Homily begins as follows:

'This day, good Christian people, shall be declared unto you the unprofitableness and shameful unhonesty of contention, strife, and debate; to the intent that, when you shall see, as it were in a table painted before your eyes, the evilfavouredness and deformity of this most detestable vice, your stomachs may be moved to rise against it, and to detest and abhor that sin, which is so much to be hated, and so pernicious and hurtful to all men. But among all kinds of contention none is more hurtful than is contention in matters of religion.... This contention and strife was in St Paul's time among the Corinthians, and is at this time among us Englishmen. For too many there be which, upon the ale benches or other places, delight to set forth certain questions, not so much pertaining to edification as to vain glory and shewing forth of their cunning; and so unsoberly to reason and dispute, that, when neither party will give place to other, they fall to chiding and contention, and sometime from hot words to further inconvenience.'

On the two preceding Sundays of this term I have ventured to call your attention to two elemental moral responsibilities under which you stand as Christians, that is to say, as members of the Church or Body of Christ, and also as Englishmen, that is to say, as members of a Commonwealth or State. These two moral responsibilities were, first, the frank recognition that you serve God and the Sovereign in a particular degree or station or sort or condition or rank, and therefore you lie under the duty of obedience; and, secondly, that you serve Christ and your King not merely in your spirits, but in your bodies, and that therefore everything that is embraced under the Greek word πορνεία and its English equivalent 'whoredom' is to be by you not smiled at or dallied with, but abhorred and repelled from you. I have ventured to set these duties before you not at all as though they were some private or peculiar notion of mine, but as they were once set before English men and women, at the instigation of Queen Elizabeth, 'according to the mind of the Holy Ghost expressed in the Scriptures' (I am here quoting from the Preface to the Homilies of the Church of England).

But there is a third moral duty under which you stand, a duty which is concerned with your manner of behaviour not so much towards your superiors or inferiors as with your behaviour towards your equals. I am referring, of course, to our duty towards our neighbours. In the Homilies almost as serious attention is paid to this as to the duties which men owe to God and to their Prince. The three are, of course, interlocked, since, if we are quarrelling among ourselves, how can we profitably range ourselves within the fabric either of Church or of State? And so it comes about that the First Book of the Homilies concludes with 'A Sermon against Contention and Brawling, in three Parts'. By 'brawling' is meant, not so much physical violence, as anger, hatred, envy, malice, faction, and all uncharitableness, and, in particular, these vices when they take shape and form in things pertaining to Christ's religion. The Queen was confronted by dangerous movements among her people, movements which were dangerous because accompanied by hot anger, and which were not merely movements but factions. In this situation she commanded the Church to speak, and here again she bade the Church speak of its proper theme and with its proper authority. And in the Homily against Strife and Contention the Church does throw itself back on quite final moral issues and speak with quite final moral authority. The Homily does not speak of toleration or of uniformity, nor of any weak and careless submission to the opinions of others. It is assumed that there will be and must be controversy, and even that there will and must at times be harshness in dealing with other people. What the Homily is concerned with is the moral framework in which controversy and firmness ought to take place and by which they must be circumscribed if they are not to degenerate into faction and brawling. Nor does it speak of this framework as though it were a limitation imposed by some kind of worldly wisdom or secular system of ethics: the limitation upon our angry behaviour is imposed by Christ upon all who believe in Him, and to this the Homily appeals. It is concerned to bring Christians under the divine command of Charity.

'If', so runs the last paragraph of the third Part of the Homily, 'we have forsaken the devil, let us use no more devilish tongues. He that hath been a railing scolder, now let him be a sober counsellor. He that hath been a malicious slanderer, now let him be a loving comforter. He that hath been a vain railer, now let him be a ghostly teacher. He that hath abused his tongue in cursing, now let him use it in blessing. He that hath abused his tongue in evil speaking, now let him use it in speaking well.... If you may, an it be possible, in no wise be angry. But, if you may not be clean void of this passion, then yet so temper and bridle it, that it stir you not to contention and brawling.'

These are no doubt rough words, but can we rightly persuade ourselves that the things against which the Homily is speaking are not to be found among us as well in matters of secular as of religious dispute? You will most assuredly be compelled to play your part in con-

troversial matters, and you will not be able to avoid
controversy concerning the meaning of Christ's religion.
It is imperative, therefore, that you should rightly
understand what Christian Charity means, and what it
does not mean.

First, all this Christian language about love and
meekness and submission does not mean that you are to
be rid of everything that is virile and masculine. Listen
to the Homily on this point.

'If I be evil reviled, shall I stand still, like a goose
or a fool, with my finger in my mouth? Shall I be
such an idiot and dizzard to suffer every man to
speak upon me what they list, to rail what they list,
to spew out all their venom against me at their
pleasures?'

To these questions the author of the Homily replies
by pointing out that it is not the mark of a strong man
merely to render evil for evil. He that in such a situation
'cannot temper nor rule his own anger is but weak and
feeble, and rather more like a woman or a child than a
strong man: for the true strength and manliness is to
overcome wrath, and to despise injury and other men's
foolishness'.

Christian Charity means that it is better to be
reviled than to be so weak as to fume and chafe in
return, for this often does but suggest that we are in fact
guilty of the thing of which we have been accused.

But there are other things which the Christian man
must bear in mind when his neighbour has offended him.

'Call thou to thy remembrance with how many
words and deeds, how grievously, thou hast offended

thy Lord God. What was man when Christ died for him? Was he not his enemy, and unworthy to have his favour and mercy? Even so with what gentleness and patience doth he forbear and tolerate and suffer thee, although he is daily offended by thee!'

And so, even when we are manifestly in the right, we must not forget that it is not always so. Thus Charity means that we should reason with ourselves after this sort:

> 'He spake these words, but it was in a sudden heat; or the drink spake them, and not he; or he spake them at the motion of some other; or he spake them being ignorant of the truth; he spake them not against me, but against him whom he thought me to be.'

This is Charity, and this is the Christian framework in which we must live with our neighbours and conduct our controversies with them, lest we should get ourselves into the position of speaking well of no man, and therefore of speaking evil of all men.

But there is another side to all this, and this other side is relevant to the meaning which is assigned to the Christian duty of Charity. Our Lord held His peace when He was called a Samaritan, a carpenter's son, and a wine-bibber, but He spoke sternly and humbly when He heard men say of Him, 'Thou hast a devil'. There is therefore 'a time when it is convenient to *answer a fool according to his own foolishness, lest he should seem in his own conceit to be wise*'. Listen to the Homily here:

> 'When our infamy (or the reproach that is done unto us) is joined with the peril of many, then it is

necessary in answering to be quick and ready. For we read that many holy men of good zeal have sharply and fiercely both spoken and answered tyrants and evil men; which sharp words came not of anger, rancour, or malice, or desire of vengeance, but of a fervent desire to bring them to the true knowledge of God and from ungodly living by an earnest and sharp rebuke and chiding.'

And yet, though it is necessary for this to be said, we must exercise great care here, and it will be well if we end with the warning that of contention and malice riseth much evil, which is so hurtful to the society of a commonwealth, that 'in all well ordered cities...common brawlers and scolders be punished with a notable kind of pain'.

VIII. OF THE MISERY OF ALL MANKIND

'O earth, earth, earth, hear the word of the Lord.'
                              (Jeremiah xxii. 29.)
'I myself also am a mortal man, like to all,
And am sprung from one born of the earth,...
and in the womb of a mother was I moulded into
    flesh....
For no king had any other first beginning. But all men
    have one entrance into life and a like departure.'
                        (Wisdom of Solomon vii. 1 ff.)

On Wednesday next, being Ash Wednesday, the first day of Lent, the Communion will be celebrated in this

Chapel at eight o'clock, and the Commination Service will be read at ten o'clock.

At both these services we shall be reminded that the Word of the Lord is spoken to mortal men, or, using the language of the Bible and the Prayer Book, to dust and ashes, to sinful men, even to miserable sinners. Only in this context is the Gospel of the Church anything but a meaningless Gospel; only in the Scriptural context of sin and mortality, of dust and ashes, has the Christian word 'Salvation' any meaning at all.

It is, however, precisely this framework of the Gospel which is to-day almost universally denied. The optimistic language of the Church has passed into modern orthodoxy in some form or other, and we speak of freedom, of liberty, of equality, of life, and of the love of God; but, because we have forgotten and blotted out the grim background of faith, our optimism is in grave danger of becoming both trivial and cruel. Trivial, because if we use of ourselves language which is properly relevant only to angels, we are manifestly talking nonsense; cruel, because, if we be accustomed to think of ourselves as other than of the earth, we have no protection against the rough things of earth, and if we are unprotected, we shall be disappointed and needlessly unhappy. As the Psalmist says, 'Destruction and unhappiness is in their ways, and the way of peace have they not known': 'There were they brought in great fear, even where no fear was.' And, trusting in ourselves, we shall then 'mock at the counsel of the poor, because he putteth his trust in the Lord'. But the poor will be right, and we shall be wrong, however grand our idealism may seem to be.

There is much unhappiness abroad to-day, and in its

more subtle forms it is, I think, nearly always the consequence of a failure to face up squarely and honestly to the fact of mortality and to the consequent limitations within which human life has to be lived. There is much battering of heads against impenetrable walls, much anger that there is no place of exit to the free air of unfettered personal liberty. And this anger, this battering of heads is painful and exhausting.

Nondum considerasti quanti ponderis sit peccatum: 'Thou hast not yet taken into account how heavy is the weight of sin.' With these words St Anselm demanded of the readers of his tract *Cur Deus homo* that they should reconsider the grounds upon which alone Christian faith can appear credible and consistent. Nor is St Anselm here unique, for every fresh appreciation of the meaning of Christianity has had its starting-point in a new and serious recognition that we are of the earth, earthy, mortal. 'Earth, earth, earth, hear the word of the Lord.' There are not lacking signs that the Church is once again being thrust back upon its proper foundations. It may not then be inconvenient if on this Sunday before Ash Wednesday we turn our attention to the most difficult and yet the most characteristic of the Homilies, to the Homily entitled, 'A Sermon of the Misery of all Mankind'.

I do not dare read to you the sub-title* of this Homily, lest you should be too gravely shocked.

In the First Book of Homilies the theme of the misery of mankind precedes all other themes, save that of the profitable necessity of the knowledge of the Bible. The 'Fruitful Exhortation to the Reading and Knowledge of

---

* ['and of his Condemnation to Death Everlasting by his own Sin.'— ED.]

Holy Scripture' is the first Homily, and it is followed at once by the Homily with which we are now concerned.

There is, I think, no doubt that our understanding of the sixteenth century is stretched when it is recognised how deeply the sense of sin and of mortality affected the religious language of the Reformation. Our own Prayer Book echoes it, for the ancient structure of the Church's worship is broken again and again to make room for the deep-seated cry for forgiveness. The opening words of the Litany—'O God the Father of heaven, have mercy upon us miserable sinners'; the prefatory sentences to Mattins and Evensong, 'I acknowledge my transgressions, and my sin is ever before me', followed at once by the General Confession, 'Almighty and most merciful Father, we have erred and strayed from thy ways like lost sheep'; the repeated breaking of the movement of the Communion Office in order to emphasise the sin of those who worship, the reading of the Ten Commandments, the exhortation, 'Ye that do truly and earnestly repent you of your sins', the comfortable words, 'Come unto me all ye that labour and are heavy laden', the Prayer of Humble Access, 'We do not presume to come to this thy table trusting in our own righteousness': all this interruption of the steady movement of the Liturgy marks the period of the Reformation. Not, of course, that it is some new thing, for it is both a Biblical and a Catholic emphasis, but the Reformers clearly intended that it should nowhere be overlooked or hidden out of sight.

To us this language seems nervous, strained and unhealthy, and particularly so when the word 'miserable' is so frequently used. But the Reformers were on the whole neither nervous, nor strained, nor unhealthy, and they were certainly not miserable, in the ordinary modern sense of the word. The Reformers were fighting a battle: and since it is almost certain that we shall have to fight the same battle, it may not be waste of time for us to attempt to discuss what they were in fact talking about.

It is here that the Homily 'of the Misery of all Mankind', in spite of its forbidding title and far more repellent sub-title, is, nevertheless, important.

The Homily begins as follows:

'The Holy Ghost, in writing the holy Scripture, is in nothing more diligent than to pull down man's vainglory and pride; which of all vices is most universally grafted in all mankind.... In the book of Genesis Almighty God giveth us all a title and name in our great-grandfather Adam, which ought to warn us all to consider what we be, whereof we be, from whence we came, and whither we shall [go], saying thus: *In the sweat of thy face shalt thou eat thy bread, till thou be turned again into the ground; for out of it wast thou taken; inasmuch as thou art dust, and into dust shalt thou be turned again.* Here, as it were in a glass, we may learn to know ourselves to be but ground, earth, and ashes, and that to earth and ashes we shall return.'

The writer of the Homily then goes on to show that the Scriptures everywhere require the open recognition before God of the frailty of human nature in itself and by itself and of itself. Judith, Esther, Job, and the Prophet Jeremiah

'called and cried to God for help and mercy with such a ceremony of sackcloth, dust, and ashes, that thereby they might declare to the whole world what an humble and lowly estimation they had of themselves, and how well they remembered their name and title.... This our right name, calling, and title, *Earth, Earth, Earth*...sheweth what we be indeed, by whatsoever other style, title, or dignity men do call us.'

Nor is this designation of mortality only a theme of the Old Testament. In the New Testament it is not otherwise. John the Baptist was great before the Lord, filled even from his birth with the Holy Ghost; the forerunner of Christ, and commended of Him to be more than a prophet: yet, in spite of all this, he needed to be washed of Christ, and humbled himself as unworthy to unbuckle His shoes. Our Lord clearly preferred the penitent Publican before 'the proud, holy, and glorious Pharisee'; and when He named Himself the Physician, He meant thereby that men were sick and not whole or perfect or angels.

Thus in the first Part of the Homily this recognition of mortality is supported, surely overwhelmingly supported, from Scripture. In the second Part of the Homily it is stated, first, that the true knowledge of ourselves is very necessary if we are to come to the right knowledge of God; secondly, that we ought not to be ashamed to confess our imperfections.

'For truly there be imperfections in our best works: we do not love God so much as we are bound to do, with all our heart, mind and power; we do not fear God so much as we ought to do; we do not pray to God but with great and many imperfections; we give, forgive, believe, love, and hope unperfectly: we speak, think, and do unperfectly; we fight against the devil, the world, and the flesh unperfectly. Let us therefore not be ashamed to confess plainly our state of imperfection; yea, let us not be ashamed to confess imperfection even in all our own best works. Let none of us be ashamed to say with holy St Peter, *I am a sinful man*....Let us learn to know ourselves, our frailty and weakness, without any cracking or boasting of our own good deeds and merits. Let us also [ac]knowledge the exceeding mercy of God towards us....'

This Homily is without doubt a proper introduction to the observance of Lent and, in particular, to the keeping of Ash Wednesday. But it all sounds, I know, very pietistic, very individual, very unmodern, and it is difficult to make up one's mind whether it represents the Church of England at its best or at its worst. Most people seem to think it is the latter, and few modern clergy are bold enough to expect their congregations to gather together on Ash Wednesday to hear the Commination Service read.

And yet, are we right to think and act thus? Remember, all this language is not talking primarily about our relation to one another but about our relation to God. If we bear this in mind, are we quite certain that it is not still relevant and necessary language? Do not men and women everywhere identify their own particular propaganda with the Kingdom of God, and consequently thrust their opponents into the kingdom of the devil, and do they not thereby exalt themselves in almost intolerable fashion? And are we guiltless in this matter? Is it not, therefore, important that at least once in the year we should be reminded that our thoughts and actions, even our good thoughts and good works, are frail, relative and imperfect things, when measured by the Righteousness and Truth of God? And is it not a healthy thing that we should be reminded, at least once a year, that we are mortal creatures, lest if pride once governs our relation to God, it may corrupt our relation to other people and damage our relation to our neighbours, and finally leave us isolated, intolerable, and quite finally unhappy and miserable people? Thus understood, this Scriptural and sixteenth-century language does undoubtedly preserve an important and even fundamental truth of the Christian religion: and if the Church does not say these things and drive them home with all the authority of which it is capable, do you think it seems likely that anyone else will do so?

V

THE IMPORTANCE OF THE
PARKER MANUSCRIPTS IN
THE COLLEGE LIBRARY

(1932)

THE IMPORTANCE OF THE PARKER MANUSCRIPTS IN THE COLLEGE LIBRARY

I

'Look...to the hole of the pit whence ye were digged.'   (Isaiah li. 1.)

There are two different kinds of Librarian. There are those learned scholars whose knowledge of the books and manuscripts under their care is more profound than that even of the most learned of visitors to their Library. There are, on the other hand, Librarians who regard it as their privilege to act as the personal hosts of visiting scholars; who welcome them, and endeavour to ensure their bodily comfort.

Having no technical knowledge sufficient to qualify me for a Librarian of the learned type, I have been compelled merely to care, sometimes I am afraid inadequately, for the comfort of our visitors. But since when men are happy they are inclined to talk, I have during the past seven years picked up scraps of information which make the figure of Archbishop Parker himself almost more interesting than any of the books and manuscripts which he bequeathed to our care. Looked at from the inside of our Library he appears as a more significant figure in English history than has usually been recognised.

Why did the Archbishop regard his collection of manuscripts as of so great importance that, when he left them to the care of the Master and Fellows of this College, he tied up his gift with such stringent conditions?

Was it merely that he was a proud collector? Was he, in fact, a collector at all, as we normally understand the word? Why did he wish his manuscripts to be so carefully preserved?

Let me remind you of the conditions of his gift.

The Master and Fellows were, upon their admission, to take an oath for the safe keeping of the manuscripts.

The manuscripts were to be kept under three keys, one to be lodged with the Master, the other two with the keepers of the Billingford Chest, a fund founded in 1432 by the then Master, Richard de Billingford. That is to say, the consent of the Master and of two Fellows was required before access to the manuscripts could be secured.

Most important of all, should a certain specified number of manuscripts be lost through 'supine negligence', the whole collection was, with the consent of the Vice-Chancellor and of one senior Doctor, to be surrendered within a month to Gonville and Caius College. If they incurred similar loss the manuscripts were to go to Trinity Hall, and if Trinity Hall were likewise negligent the bequest reverted to us: and so forth.

The result of all this is that the collection remains unimpaired.

The Provost of Eton, in the preface to the catalogue of our manuscripts, describes the Archbishop's injunctions as 'mysterious'. I wish to put a question mark against this word 'mysterious'.

Matthew Parker was born in Norwich in 1504. He came to this College in 1521. Queen Anne Boleyn, the

mother of Queen Elizabeth, made him her chaplain in
1535. He became chaplain to Henry VIII in 1537. He
was made Master of the College in 1544. He was Vice-
Chancellor in 1544–5 and again in 1548–9.

He resigned his Mastership at the accession of Queen
Mary, and lived in seclusion during her reign. Where
he hid himself we do not know; but he did not leave the
country and migrate to Zurich or to Strassburg. On her
accession, Queen Elizabeth made him her first Archbishop of Canterbury in 1559, and he died on May 17th,
1575.

I need hardly draw attention to the disturbed state of
this country at the accession of Queen Elizabeth, and to
the dangers which threatened it from within and from
without. Confidence in the Queen and in her policy was
of vital importance, and the shaping of that policy can
have been no simple affair.

It was then that Parker took up his residence at
Lambeth. The question is, Did he contribute anything
to English confidence at that time? or, rather, Did he
attempt to provide a particular ground of confidence?

Let me put this question in another way. Was anything being done at Lambeth to give this realm of
England a sense of dignity and independence, and to
protect Elizabethan England from the accusation that
it was an innovation which rested upon no secure
foundations? Or was Parker merely an administrator
residing in his Palace at Lambeth? What was Parker's
contribution to Elizabethan England?

It is when looked at from our Library that Lambeth
Palace appears important in the particular context of
the history of the beginning of Elizabeth's reign, and

that Matthew Parker stands out as infinitely more than an administrator, or a mere collector of manuscripts.

We know that the Archbishop kept at his own expense and among his household at Lambeth scribes skilled in copying ancient manuscripts. Among our manuscripts we have whole manuscripts transcribed by these Parkerian scribes. But more than this: lacunae in our Anglo-Saxon manuscripts are filled in in a sixteenth-century Parkerian hand from other manuscripts to which Parker secured access. Moreover, our manuscripts bear marks of having been read carefully when at Lambeth, since important passages are marked with a red pencil, which was either Parker's own, or that of his secretary, Joscelin.

Further, we know that Parker had an Anglo-Saxon type cut at his own expense in order that selections from Anglo-Saxon manuscripts might be printed and circulated in England. Quite a considerable number of books were, in fact, published at the Archbishop's expense, and these books were the result of his work or the work of his scribes upon the manuscripts which he had brought together.

What is quite clear from the condition of our manuscripts is that they were not merely collected by Parker, but that they were collected for a purpose, and that they were worked upon in Lambeth under the direction of the Archbishop, also for a purpose.

That is to say, Parker's collection is not such as was made by the English aristocracy when as young men they went on the Grand Tour and returned from the Continent with a valuable collection of books and pictures and statuary which now form the bulk of the treasures of English country houses. This collection of ours was made to be used in some way for the moulding of English public opinion and for the safety of this realm of England, and was so used. Lambeth Palace was a workshop, the manuscripts were the tools used in the workshop, and Matthew Parker's was the master mind. That is to say, we have in this College something important for the understanding of Elizabethan England, and perhaps for more than that.

What manuscripts then did Parker collect? And what did he expect to find in them? And what did he, in fact, find in them?

Parker was not interested in foreign manuscripts: that, at any rate, is clear from the manuscripts he did collect. Our manuscripts are almost wholly English manuscripts written in England by Englishmen, and illuminated in England by Englishmen, and reaching back to the Anglo-Saxon period and to the reign of King Alfred. Fuller was certainly right when he described our books as 'the sun of English antiquity'.

The destruction of the monasteries involved the scattering of the great libraries of St Augustine's and Christchurch at Canterbury, Winchester, St Albans, and Bury St Edmunds, libraries which contained the records of English history. For some thirty to forty years these books had disappeared into private hands. It was Parker who set to work to recover what was recoverable, and for this purpose he employed men to search for them. But it cannot have been that he merely wished to secure any ancient book. What he wanted chiefly were those books which threw light on the ancient condition of England, and upon the history of England.

Our collection represents a most careful and critical selection.

Fortunately, that Parker had a particular purpose is not a matter of conjecture but is now definitely established. A few weeks ago, one of the Canons of Hereford on going through the Chapter Book came upon a letter of Parker's written on January 20th, 1565, to Bishop Scory, then Bishop of Hereford. The relevant passage runs thus:

> 'I give you thanks that you did not forget to cause Hereford Library to be searched for Saxon Books whereof ye make mention to me. Praying your Lordship to cause them to be sent unto me by the carryar to have the use of them for a tyme, meaning with thanks shortly to return them again. Or if any other *old historye* of England be in the same library or in your own store.'

Then a note in the hand of one of the Canons:

> 'These books—3—were sent to my L. Bp. of Hereford. Feb. 8. 1565.'

The story is completed, for we have a letter from Bishop Scory saying that he has sent the Archbishop three books.

Here then we have Parker's main aim in black and white. Saxon Books—Old Histories of England—and that this must have been his general aim is proved by the presence in our Library of thirty-seven Anglo-Saxon manuscripts, to which must be added seven more given by Parker to the University Library, and certainly one now in the Bodleian. That is to say, Parker must have possessed or had the use of more Anglo-Saxon books than we, at present, possess.

Then we have no less than thirty-eight chronicles of English History, including, of course, the Winchester Anglo-Saxon chronicle and the original manuscript of the Matthew Paris Chronicle with Matthew Paris' notes and additions and his marginal illuminations.

And Parker gathered together these books, as he says to Bishop Scory, *for use*.

For what precise use? What seems to me to be the inevitable particular answer to this question, I must leave until next Sunday. But meanwhile we must not overlook the general significance of our books regarded as a whole. They bear witness to the achievements of English intelligence and of English piety. And at a time when it was precisely this confidence in English attainment which was required to give Englishmen confidence in their country, and to provide a protection of soul against foreign threats to Church and State, Parker not only gained from these books a confidence to support his own position as Archbishop in the Church of England, but he was able to expound it to others both by his own words and by the books which he caused to be printed and circulated. It is these printed books which betray everywhere the debt which he owed to the manuscripts he had gathered together.

Our manuscripts not only were but are the charter of English freedom, and that is why they are not a mere collection, but are themselves, as a collection, a bit of

English history. We can never, even if we were able to do so, permit our books to be thrown into some cosmopolitan library, where they would become just isolated books and lose their corporate distinction.

II

If, then, the first impression of the Parker Manuscripts as a whole is that they were brought together as a witness to the culture and intelligence and Christianity which had existed in this country from Anglo-Saxon times, it follows that their very existence, and much more their existence as a collection in the hands of the Archbishop of Canterbury, was, consequently, a criticism of those who behaved as though truth in Religion was to be sought for by means of some importation from elsewhere.

Though it seems to me that there is a simple-hearted patriotism behind the Archbishop's vigorous collection, yet it would be false to suppose that we have to deal with no more than this. Mere patriotic pride would not explain the care with which these manuscripts were obviously studied, nor would it explain the printed books which were issued from Lambeth as a result of this investigation of the manuscripts.

We possess in the Library not only the Archbishop's collection of manuscripts, but also what we call the Small or Little Parker Books. These latter were the Archbishop's private books. Amongst them is to be found the evidence of the use which was made of the manuscripts, and what was in the Archbishop's mind when he caused the manuscripts to be worked upon, and when he himself paid for the publication of the result of this work.

Two little printed books in the Archbishop's private library and one other, which strangely enough was not amongst his books, but which was secured for the Library three years ago, together with a fourth which was presented to us some years since, throw light upon what was actually going on in Lambeth.

In 1565 a 'Student in Divinitie', Thomas Stapleton by name, translated into English the Venerable Bede's History of the Church of England. Stapleton's translation was published in Antwerp with a dedication to Queen Elizabeth and a somewhat lengthy preface in which the translator explains the reason for publishing the book. He wishes, as he says, to shew the differences between the 'Primitive faith of England continued almost through a thousand years and the pretended faith of protestants' and the book is presented to the Queen's Royal Majesty for the Realm's commodity.

This judgment of newfangledness was directed against the Church of England at the beginning of Elizabeth's reign, and it was a very serious attack, since it was supported by an appeal to history.

This attack by Stapleton was, of course, typical, and you will all recognise that the religious situation at the beginning of Elizabeth's reign was very delicate and difficult, and books like that of Stapleton threatened to foment already existing disunion. If the Church of England were merely newfangled, it might attract to itself those who were governed in their religion by the great continental centres of Protestantism, but it would hardly satisfy the vast majority of Englishmen. This uncertainty of the position of the Church of England was a great weakness not only ecclesiastically but in the whole architectural structure of this realm.

Now, it was to this apparent weakness of the Church of England that the Archbishop addressed himself, and it was in order to answer the charge of newfangledness and to awaken confidence in the Church of England that he collected our manuscripts and embarked upon this investigation.

The wealth both of Biblical manuscripts and of early commentaries upon the Bible, which are included among our manuscripts, is no doubt due to one great and important line of defence of the Church of England. The study of the Bible and of its meaning to the early Fathers of the Church, which was an appeal to sound Biblical scholarship, enabled Parker to claim that many changes could be explained and justified by the authority of the Bible and of its earliest interpretation in the Primitive Church. Important and interesting as this Biblical appeal is, since it laid the foundation of that steady Biblical work which has been a characteristic feature of the Church of England from that day to this, it is not to this that I wish at this moment to draw your attention.

More peculiar and perhaps more interesting in the light of our Library is the answer which Parker made to the charge that the changes in the old order had no authority in the history of the English Church itself. It was through the investigation of the Anglo-Saxon Church as revealed in the Anglo-Saxon manuscripts he had collected that Parker endeavoured to make his peculiar contribution to the confidence of Englishmen in the Church of England.

There were three changes for which the Church of England was most vehemently attacked as newfangled:

The general use of the Scriptures in English,
The discarding of the doctrine of Transubstantiation,
and
.The marriage of the clergy.

On all these three points very remarkable evidence came to light through the investigation of the Anglo-Saxon manuscripts.

Archbishop Parker had in his possession at least three manuscripts of the Gospels in Anglo-Saxon English, and these manuscripts seemed to have been used in the liturgy of the ancient English Church. They were, there-fore, of great importance to Parker. How important he considered them is shewn by his having these Gospels set up in Anglo-Saxon type and printed, flanked by the Elizabethan version of the Gospels. The title-page runs:

'The Gospels of the Fower Evangelists translated in the Olde Saxons tyme out of Latin into the vulgare tongue of the Saxons newly collected out of Ancient Monumentes of the said Saxons, and now published *for testimonie of the same.*'

Dated at London, 1571, and published under royal privilege.

The preface to the book, written by John Foxe, con-tains indeed the explanation of the significance of our manuscripts. I select three passages:

'What a controversy, among other controversies more, hath risen of late in our days, whether it be convenient the Scriptures of God to be put in our English tongue. Wherein some more confidently than skilfully, contrary both to evidence of Antiquity, as also against the open face of veritie, have thought it to be dangerous to have them in our popular language translated, considering partly the difficultie of the Scriptures in themselves, and partly the weakness of understanding in us. Some again have judged our native tongue unmeet to express God's secret mysteries, being so barbarous and imperfect a language, as they say it is.'

This is then answered by the publication of the Saxon translation:

'As touching this our Realm of England, if any shall doubt of the ancient usage thereof, whether they had the Scriptures in their language of old times, here he may have a proofe of so much translated into our old English tongue, the divers translations whereof... be yet extant to be seen as well long before the Conquest as since.

'Therefore we have published this treatise especially to this end, that the said book, imprinted thus in the Saxons letters, may remain in the Church as a profitable example and precedent of old antiquitie *to the more confirmation of your* (Queen Elizabeth's) gratious proceedings now in the Church agreeable to the same.

'Wherein we are beholden to the reverend and learned father in God, Matthew, Archbishop of Canterbury, a cheefe and a famous travailler in this

Church of England, by whose industrious diligence
and learned labours this book, with others more have
been collected and searched out of the Saxon monu-
ments.'

Now comes the key to the whole procedure, clearly
expressed:

'We understand by the edition hereof, how the
religion presently taught and professed in the Church
at thys present, is no new reformation of things lately
begun, but rather a reduction of the Church to the
Pristine State...as is manifestly proved not onely in
this case of the vulgar translation of the Scriptures;
but in other cases also in doctrine, as Transubstantiation, of priests restrained from marriage, of receiving
under one kind, with many other points and articles
newly thrust in.'

I have illustrated in some detail the use made of the
Anglo-Saxon manuscripts in handling the question of
the use of the Scriptures in English. But under the
guidance of the Archbishop the same procedure was
adopted in dealing with the doctrine of Transubstantiation and with the question of the marriage of priests.

Two Anglo-Saxon homilies were printed in Anglo-
Saxon with a translation, one 'on the Sacrament of the
Body and Blood of Christ our Saviour, appointed in the
reign of the Saxons to be spoken unto the people before
they should receive the Communion', and the second on
reservation for the sick, the latter printed with the
signatures of the Archbishop and twelve other Bishops.
The point of this was to shew that in the Anglo-Saxon
Church there was, apparently, no knowledge of the

medieval doctrine of transubstantiation, and that the Elizabethan Church should not be accused of innovation if that teaching was not taught.

Similarly with the marriage of priests. The Archbishop was able to quote from the early English Chronicles to shew that the Anglo-Saxon clergy were, in fact, married, and indeed the Archbishop writes in his book entitled *A Defence of Priests' Marriages* that Henry of Huntingdon says in his Chronicle that during the Archbishopric of Anselm the Archbishop held a council in London at the which he forbade priests to have wives (which were never before forbidden), which things seemed to some most pure, to others dangerous.

And now, in conclusion, surely there is no difficulty in understanding why Matthew Parker regarded his collection of manuscripts as of national importance. They were of vital importance for the defence and understanding of the Church of England.

There is, then, no mystery about his careful regulations for their preservation.

APPENDIX
A LETTER FROM ENGLAND*

CORPUS CHRISTI COLLEGE,
CAMBRIDGE,
Tuesday in Holy Week, 1936

My dear Colleague!

We have, as you know, never met. It is true, we have corresponded; but even our correspondence has been a very pedestrian affair, confined chiefly to the finding of a proper equivalent in English for a difficult word or sentence or allusion in your exposition of the Epistle to the Romans. This limited personal relationship between two theologians is not to be regretted, and very particularly not to be regretted when the responsibility of one is limited to the translation into his own language of what the other has written. We are separated by the very real barrier of a different language, a different political tradition, a different quality of piety and impiety, a different structure even of theological and untheological heritage. And you well know that there are still wider divergencies lying behind all these things, which can hardly be referred to in private, certainly not set out in print. And yet, however different the background and texture of human thought and behaviour may be, the problem of faith is the same problem, the problems of theology are the same problems,—and the answer is the same answer.

---

* Reprinted from *Theologische Aufsätze: Karl Barth zum 50. Geburtstag* (Chr. Kaiser Verlag, München, 1936), pp. 525–7.

To have recognized this is to have apprehended the situation in which theologians stand together and side by side. You will therefore perhaps understand and forgive me if, for one moment, I break through the reserve that has been imposed upon us, in order to assure you that your work has not been altogether misunderstood in England, and to assure you also that your purpose in permitting your book to appear in English has not been altogether overlooked: you said at the end of the preface to the English version of your exposition of the Epistle to the Romans, "Theology is *ministerium verbi divini*. It is nothing more nor less. The conflict in which we have been engaged in Germany during the past ten years revolves round the apprehension of this truth. My purpose in permitting this commentary upon the Epistle of Paul to the Romans to appear in English is to summon an ever increasing number of men to engage themselves in this conflict."

What I have to say must be quite short; and will seem to many of your friends most inadequate, but it will, I hope, not be so to you.

1. There are many in England, laymen and clergy and ministers, who know what you meant when you said what you did say to them at the conclusion of your preface.

2. For us, as for you in Central Europe, the subject-matter of the Bible is difficult, strange and foreign. Yet in our aloofness we know that its relevance lies in its strangeness, and that we are involved in its definition of human life. What you have written has enabled a large number of men and women in England to see this tension of far and near, this contradiction of strangeness and relevance, more clearly, and to recognize its vast importance.

3. The story of the penetration of English thought and behaviour, both inside and outside the church, by what may, for want of a better word, be described as 'humanism', and the consequent driving into the background of any strict theological, or dogmatic, or even biblical, frame of reference, is a long, a very long story. But the characteristic English substitution of piety for theology, and the inevitable revolt against this venerable piety, mean that a strain is now being placed upon our peculiar heritage which it is exceedingly doubtful whether it is able to bear. In this general context of thought and conduct, your insistence that the questions, What is theology? What is dogmatic theology? and, very particularly, What is Biblical theology? are unescapable questions, has not passed unnoticed.

4. We have reached a point where once again we too are compelled to ask questions. Can the church, can indeed human society, remain satisfied to go on its way untroubled by the relevance of what apostles and prophets once said? Can we theologians be satisfied to pick up fragments of what they said, to set these fragments in a non-biblical, non-theological, and ultimately inhuman setting; and then hand them out in that form to clergy and laity alike? Or again, Is a theological faculty in a university true to its subject-matter, if it never be permitted to stray beyond a purely historical description of the church in primitive and other times, or, if it be permitted to stray, to stray only into speculative theology? These and many other such-like problems —all of them, however, but different aspects of one central theme, the theme of revelation—are our problems as well as yours. And what you have said and done has made these problems, if not more acute, at any rate more widely recog-

nized. We too know that we are standing where those men once stood to whom apostles and evangelists and prophets once spoke, and that therefore we have to take seriously what they said. Here again, what you, in defining this position and in declaring that it is the position of us all, have said, has been of great importance for us in England, and will be, I think, of even greater importance, indirectly if not directly, in the future.

And lastly: There are some in England who are grateful to you for having so consistently reminded them that their theological and ministerial work should be of a properly scriptural quality and temper, and that their business is, as Pusey once told the Church of England, to set forth the meaning of Holy Scripture itself, to "extract" Truth from, not to "import" truths into it. There are some also who owe to you the power of speech, the recognition that their work must be accompanied by that utterance in word or writing and action which is rid of every desire for personal notoriety or for the triumph of a school of thought, because it is a cry *de profundis*, and which, by echoing the Epistle for this day— *Qui ambulavit in tenebris, et non est lumen ei*—bears witness to the glory of God and to His love of men through Jesus Christ our Lord.

Yours very sincerely

EDWYN C. HOSKYNS